PLAYING FOR TIME
The Death Row All Stars

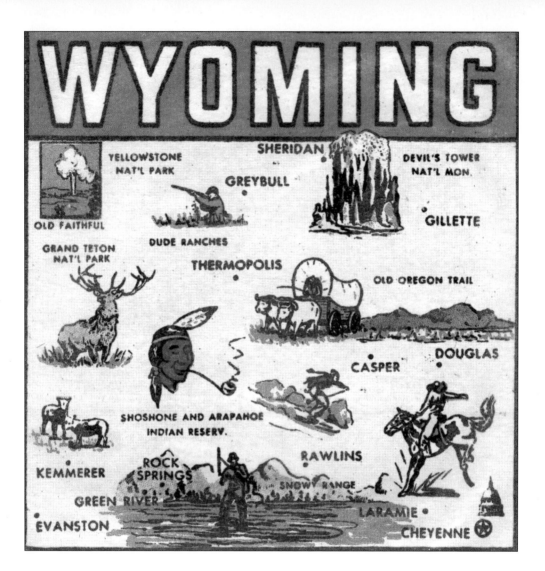

WYOMING

YELLOWSTONE NAT'L PARK

OLD FAITHFUL

GREYBULL

SHERIDAN

DEVIL'S TOWER NAT'L MON.

GILLETTE

DUDE RANCHES

GRAND TETON NAT'L PARK

THERMOPOLIS

OLD OREGON TRAIL

SHOSHONE AND ARAPAHOE INDIAN RESERV.

CASPER

DOUGLAS

KEMMERER

ROCK SPRINGS

RAWLINS

SNOWY RANGE

GREEN RIVER

EVANSTON

LARAMIE

CHEYENNE

PLAYING FOR TIME
The Death Row All Stars

Chris Enss

ARCADIA

Published by Arcadia Publishing
Charleston SC, Chicago IL, Portsmouth NH, San Francisco CA

Printed in Great Britain

Library of Congress Catalog Card Number: 2004110103

For all general information contact Arcadia Publishing at:
Telephone 843-853-2070
Fax 843-853-0044
E-mail sales@arcadiapublishing.com
For customer service and orders:
Toll-Free 1-888-313-2665

Visit us on the internet at http://www.arcadiapublishing.com

On the cover: (*background*) The All Stars practicing at the baseball field on the prison grounds.

(*front*) In this team photo from 1911, the Wyoming State Penitentiary All Stars look much like other teams of the day. The child seated in the center of the photo is Felix Alston, Jr., the son of the prison warden. He believed having his son as the mascot brought the team good luck.

(*inset*) Prisoner number 1612 was Joseph Seng, who was the best player on the team. Many thought he had the talent to play in the major leagues. On death row because, as the warden said, "He unloaded a revolver into a man's head," Seng at the end thought of his days playing ball for the All Stars as the first productive part of his life.

(*back*) The Wyoming State Penitentiary, as it looked in 1905. Called by inmates the "Crossbar Hotel," the prison housed some of the most notorious criminals of the old west, including Butch Cassidy and Frank James.

CONTENTS

ACKNOWLEDGMENTS

I happened onto the story of death row inmate baseball players while doing research on women of the old west. I was fascinated with the notion of ruthless prisoners excelling in a civilized game to the point that they became amateur sport's heroes. My interest on the subject was further enhanced when I learned of the motivation behind the Wyoming State Penitentiary All Stars wins. I was compelled to tell the story of this unique team and of the key player that led them to many victories.

Like many controversial events in history, there are as many experts to confirm the happenings as those who deny it ever occurred. The challenge facing the reporting of such a story is in the sifting through numerous contradicting reports. In spite of the criticism I have received from historians and scholars, I have chosen to tell this tale using the reports that suggest the activity of giving stays of execution to exceptional convict ball players. The idea of delaying a trip to the gallows by defeating rival baseball teams is riveting and had to be written about.

This book would not have been possible without the help of the staff at the Carbon County Museum and the Wyoming State Archives Department in Cheyenne. Territorial historian Lowell Evers services were invaluable as he helped to gather many of the photographs included in these pages. I am indebted to his expertise and wisdom. I would also like to extend my appreciation to my mother, Pat Enss, who accompanied me on the research trip to Wyoming and supported me through the writing process. And finally, to the editorial team at Arcadia Publishing for daring to bring this material to life.

INTRODUCTION

The tired pitcher stepped back off the rubber, picked up the rosin bag laying beside it, and looked around at his fielders. They were all slapping their mitts and shouting encouragement to him. He wiped the beads of sweat off his forehead with the sleeve of his jersey, took a deep breath and stepped back on the rubber. His long arms rose over his head as he started his wind-up. Rearing back on his left leg he fired a wild, high fastball. The batter turned from the plate as he faded backwards trying to avoid the out of control pitch, but the ball ricocheted off his left shoulder and bounded back into the stands.

A fat, unkempt umpire shouted for the batter to take his base. The crowd in the stands hissed at the now rattled pitcher. He cast a glance at the team captain near the dugout and noticed the grim expression on the man's face. Such a mistake would cost the pitcher his life. His shoulders sagged under the weight of the consequences of his actions.

At the conclusion of the game the pitcher wandered off the mound and joined the other players on his losing team as they lined up single file along the third base line.

A half dozen burly, heavily armed guards approached the ball club, carrying a long link of handcuffs and shackles for their legs. With guns leveled at the outfit, each player slipped the braces on and locked them in place.

Mesmerized onlookers watched the team as they were escorted off the field and loaded onto a bus. They watched the players take their seats and peer out at them through barred windows.

The Wyoming State Penitentiary All Stars games always ended with the club being led off the grounds bound in irons. Although the prisoners that made up the team played the game of baseball with civility and respect, outside of the sport their behavior was judged unruly and barbaric. Imprisoned for a variety of brutal crimes, these men were death row inmates with a gift for America's favorite pastime.

In 1911, baseball was one of the most popular and profitable activities in the state of Wyoming. Large wagers were placed on amateur league organizations like the Cheyenne Devils, the Laramie Wolverines, and the Rock Springs Mavericks; and large crowds filled the stands rooting for their prized teams and star players.

The Wyoming State Penitentiary All Stars' incentive to play and play well was two-fold. The game broke the monotony of life behind bars with an activity that was eagerly welcomed by the community, and, if the team excelled at the sport and beat all their competitors, they received stays of execution.

The All Stars most valuable player in the five year history of the ball club was a right fielder and sometime short-stop named Joseph Seng. The 29-year-old man from Pennsylvania was incarcerated for the shooting death of his employer and sentenced to be hung by the neck. Inside the walls of the penitentiary, dressed in the standard issue dark blue pants and a light gray work shirt, Seng quietly took his place among the general population of more than 500 prisoners. On the baseball diamond he set himself apart from the other inmates, excelling as a powerful hitter and gifted fielder. He led his team to victory more than once and was ultimately the driving force that helped propel the All Stars into the Amateur Western Division Championship competition.

Residents of the city of Rawlins, where the state prison was located, filled the stands of public stadiums to watch the All Stars play against the top teams in the area. They would cheer and applaud as the death row inmates poured onto the field dressed in their white-trimmed, dark blue game uniforms to take their positions. Fans chanted Seng's name and waved banners hailing him as the "Best in the West."

The criminals on the diamond always tipped their hats to the loyal spectators and, for a brief time, they rose above their offenses and dedicated themselves solely to the art of baseball. They played not only for love of the game, but ultimately for love of life.

The existence of Joseph Seng and the Wyoming State Penitentiary All Stars cannot by disputed. The facts surrounding the treatment of the team members, and the alleged gambling on their games by political figures, has been argued by many scholars. But all agree, at the very least, it's a dandy rumor.

The Wyoming State Penitentiary All Stars were a superior baseball team made up of death row inmates. As long as they won their games against civilian teams, like the Rock Springs Mavericks,

The Wyoming State Penitentiary, affectionately known as "The Crossbar Hotel," is seen here in a 1905 postcard. The prison was in operation from 1901 to 1981 and housed some of the West's most notorious outlaws. In post-Civil War Wyoming, outlaws roamed the windswept high plains, canyons, and mountains. In anticipation of statehood, the territorial legislature planned a state-of-the-art penitentiary.

they received stays of execution. The panoramic view of a stadium in Rock Springs, Wyoming shows the All Stars at bat and the Mavericks waiting in the field.

This team photo of the Wyoming State Penitentiary All Stars was taken in 1911. The child seated the center of the hardened criminals is the prison warden's five-year-old son, Felix Alston, Jr. Felix Alston, Sr. believed that having his son as the team mascot was good luck. (Photo courtesy of the Wyoming State Archives Department.)

The Wyoming State Penitentiary All Stars practice the art of baseball behind stone walls and locked gates. In 1911 and 1912 the team posted an impressive combined 39-6 record.

The Old Pen, as the Wyoming Frontier Prison is affectionately called today, is seen here in 1940. It is "haunted by history" around every corner. The prison is located at 500 West Walnut Street and is open to the public from April through October.

This is a photo of the inside of the prison as it looks today in its current use as a museum. (Photograph courtesy of the Wyoming State Penitentiary.)

ONE

Baseball Out West

"In the far and mighty West, where the crimson sun rests, there's a growing splendid state
that lies above, on the breast of this great land; where the massive Rockies stand."
—*State Song of Wyoming*

Settlers of the big plains of Wyoming loudly sang praises of the territory's beauty the day the area
was admitted to the union in March of 1890. Carved from sections of the Dakota, Utah, and
Idaho territories, Wyoming Territory came into existence by an act of Congress on July 25, 1868.

Pioneers began trekking across the spectacular landscape of the State soon after gold was
discovered in California. Landmarks such as Devil's Tower and Independence Rock, looming
prominently over the Belle Fourche River, helped guide stalwart explorers and travelers
pushing their way West. Wyoming's South Pass became famous as the easiest way for emigrants
to travel across the mountains.

Wyoming owes its early settlement in part to the gentlemen of Europe. Their fondness for
beaver top hats sent early-day trappers to the Rocky Mountains in search of prized pelts. Famous
men such as Kit Carson, Jim Bridger, Davey Jackson, and Jedediah Smith were among the
trappers and traders who made the territory their home.

Ambitious ranchers lingering in the area recognized the grazing lands the state possessed to
be the best for cattle. Soon sheepherders cast their covetous eyes on it too. And so was born a
classic hostility of the Old West.

Clashes with Native Americans, who inhabited the land prior to the white man's
encroachment, added to the volatile climate of the emerging frontier. The government sent
soldiers into the country to protect wagon trains from the hostile Indians. Military posts soon
dotted the landscape and served as a haven for Pony Express riders and Overland stage coaches
as well as the soon to come steam engine.

Tracks for the Transcontinental and the Union Pacific Railroads were completely laid across
the state in 1868. Depots sprang up and new towns were created to accommodate the iron horse
and the increasing Wyoming population. Rowdy groups of citizens took up residence in such
wild railroad stops as Battle and Rambler.

Political leaders for the 44th State had their hands full keeping the Indians appeased,
protecting settlers and businesses, and bringing law to a savage territory.

The town of Rawlins, located north of the Colorado border near the Red Desert, was one of
many railroad towns that lay along the tracks like beads on a string. Rawlins' city founders
would later help provide the state with a place to house ruffians, Indians and whites alike, who

fought against civilized behavior. Eight years after Wyoming was added to the union, the Frontier Prison was built.

Rawlins had a reputation for dealing harshly with criminals. Desperados caught in the act of robbery, rape or murder in Rawlins were not only hanged, but some were actually skinned. Various items were made from the hides of these unfortunate lawbreakers, sold as souvenirs and used as a warning to other would-be felons. When Wyoming's Ninth Legislative Assembly decided to construct a prison to house felons, there was no question that the structure should be erected in or near the city with the toughest stance on fugitives.

In 1888, Wyoming territory leaders purchased land north of Rawlins from the Union Pacific Railroad Company, and construction on the state penitentiary began. Legislative appropriations and poor weather conditions stalled building efforts over an eleven year period.

The Wyoming State Penitentiary finally opened its doors to its first customers in 1901. The prison had 104 cells, and was void of electricity and running water. Over the next ten years, improvements and modifications were made to the building, adding cells, concrete towers, and a dungeon for the punishment of unruly inmates. Convicts and prison officials alike referred to the jail as the "Crossbar Hotel."

In operation for some 80 years, the prison was home to some of the West's most notorious bad guys. Famous outlaws like Butch Cassidy and Frank James served time at the hotel. Notorious female prisoners like prostitute Dolly Brady and thieves like the Smith Sisters were also interned there.

The most popular recreational activity in Rawlins in the early 1900s, in and out of the prison, was baseball. The United States was obsessed with the game and Wyoming was one of the sport's biggest supporters. In Rawlins, like everywhere else, children and adults came together to form teams and begin playing the popular "bat and ball" game.

Wyoming State Penitentiary warden Felix Alston was fascinated with baseball and decided to organize his own team. Suggesting that an athletic program be established for the inmates, Alston began assembling players as soon as the idea was approved by the prison board.

In early 1911, the Wyoming State Penitentiary All Stars marched onto the exercise yard to begin practice. From the onset the prisoners who played the game did so with gusto and an even temperament. They worked together as one cohesive unit, making the sport look like the easiest game in the world. Prison guards spread the word about the All Stars exceptional skill and soon amateur teams from all over the state were requesting a scrimmage with the convicts.

Alston reveled in the attention his team received. Local government officials who deemed the prison athletic program a success encouraged Alston to "keep up the good work." Alston wanted an unbeatable team and set his sites on shaping the club to be just that.

By the summer of 1911, Rawlins, Wyoming was not only known for their strict treatment of lawbreakers, but as home to one of the most exceptional baseball outfits in the West.

Here is a scenic view of Carbon County, Wyoming. The name Wyoming was adopted from two Delaware Indian words, *Meche* and *Weaming*. To the Indians it meant "at the big plains," or "on the great plain."

The front entrance of the Wyoming State Penitentiary is pictured in 1905, just a few years before the players on the All Stars were to check in to the "Crossbar Hotel."

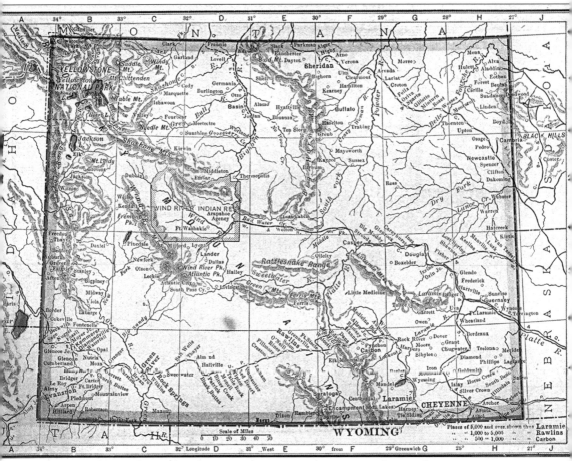

This map of Wyoming is dated 1911. The Great Plains meet the Rocky Mountains in Wyoming, a great plateau broken by a number of important mountain ranges. Many outlaws took refuge in those ranges, eluding the law sometimes for years.

Tracks laid by Union Pacific Railroad employees made access through Wyoming's rugged terrain possible.

The town of Rawlings was built up around the Union Pacific Railroad depot stop, as seen here in 1910.

BIRD'S-EYE VIEW OF RAWLINS, WYO.

The rough and tumble town of Rawlins sprawled out against the mountainous Wyoming terrain. The Wyoming State Penitentiary is to the far left of the photo, near the water tower.

The cornerstone for the penitentiary is seen here being hauled by teams of men and horses from the quarry.

The prison guard building overlooked the gallows. Seen here as it looked from outside, it appears as a typical prison guard tower. keeping an ever watchful eye on the prisoners below.

George Parrott (alias Big Nose George) was a member of a gang who attempted to rob a Union Pacific train. He shot and killed two Carbon County deputy sheriffs and was lynched and hung for the murders by Rawlins citizens on March 26, 1881.

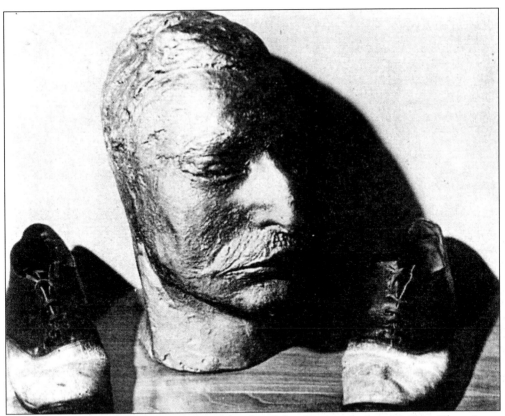

This is a plaster cast of Big Nose George's head and the shoes made from his skin. These items were put on display in the window of a popular barber shop to remind local of the price to be paid for breaking the law.

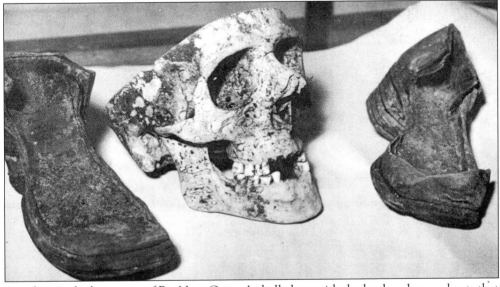

Seen here is the lower part of Big Nose George's skull along with the leather shoes or boots that were cut off his feet after he was hung in Rawlins.

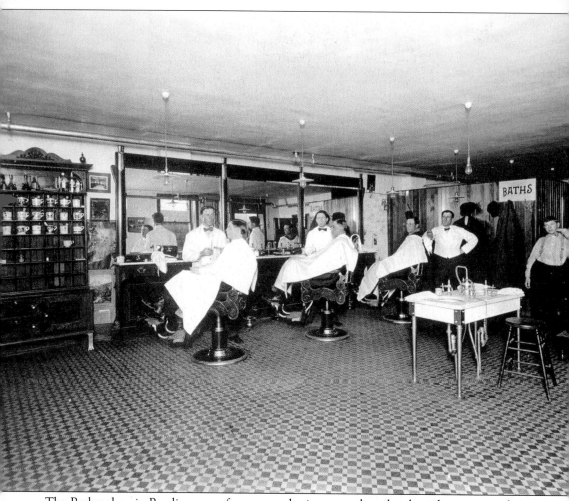

The Barber shop in Rawlins was a frequent gathering spot where local residents met to discuss the prison baseball team. It is seen here with a full house c. 1911.

WYOMING STATE PENITENTIARY RAWLINS, WY.			Name	*J. Cassidy*	No. *18*
			Alias	*B.*	
			Crime	*Grand Larceny*	
HEIGHT	HEAD LENGTH	L FOOT	Age *27*	Height *5 ft. 9 in.*	
			Weight *165*	Build *Good*	
OUTER ARMS	HEAD WIDTH	L. MIDDLE FINGER	Hair *Dark-Flaxen* Eyes *Blue*		
			Complexion *Light* Moustache		
TRUNK	CHEEK WIDTH	L. LITTLE FINGER	Born	*Utah*	
	R. EAR LENGTH	L. FOREARM	Occupation *Cowboy*		
			Arrested		
			Received from *Fremont County*		
FINGER PRINT			Sentenced *July 15 1894 / 2 yrs*		

REMARKS: *Single — No Religion — Intemperate — Common Ed.*
Released Jany 19 1896 by reason of pardon granted by Gov. Richards.

YAWMAN & ERBE MFG. CO., ROCHESTER, N. Y.   475587   1000 11-09.   P. 79

Legendary outlaw and now nearly mythic figure of the old west, Robert LeRoy Parker (better known as Butch Cassidy) was incarcerated at the Wyoming State Penitentiary in 1894. This is his mug shot and intake form from the day he checked in to the Crossbar Hotel on July 15th, 1894, at the age of 27. He was released on January 20, 1896 after serving time for horse theft.

Dolly Brandy was one of 11 female prisoners who had an extended stay at the Crossbar Hotel.

This row of cells in the interior of the Wyoming State Penitentiary gives some idea of how claustrophobic the conditions were. The cells measured a mere five by seven feet, and the penitentiary was often overcrowded in the early 20th century. (Photograph courtesy of the Wyoming State Penitentiary.)

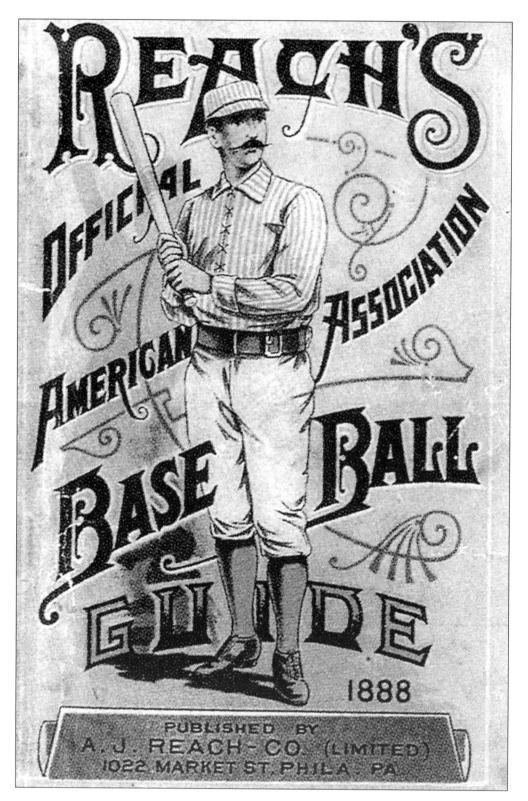

REACH'S

OFFICIAL AMERICAN ASSOCIATION BASE BALL GUIDE

1888

PUBLISHED BY
A. J. REACH - CO. (LIMITED)
1022 MARKET ST. PHILA. PA

For the general population at the Crossbar Hotel, outdoor treatment of crimes consisted of working nearby penitentiary farms and ranches. In stark contrast to the All Stars, these prisoners remained chained together during the entire duration of their time outside the prison walls (though the chains are not clearly visible in this photograph and the two on the next page)

(*opposite page*) Official baseball guides issued annually by Reach were precious commodities for all baseball fans of the era, giving them what they needed to know about that year's teams and players. This is the cover of the 1888 guide to the American Association, an early major league that operated from 1882 through 1891.

The Death Row All Stars may have enjoyed more freedom of movement on the ball fields than did their counterparts in the general prison population out in the work fields (*pictured above*), but they still faced an end far worse than hard labor. Bobby Guzmen (*pictured left*) was an All Star pitcher who eventually killed himself rather than being put to death.

TWO

Managing the All Stars

Felix Alston served as the Wyoming State Penitentiary warden from April 1911 to March 1919. He earned a stellar reputation in law enforcement as the Sheriff of Big Horn County, located north of Rawlins. He was elected to oversee range disputes between cattlemen and sheepherders and led the investigation to track down and arrest seven men responsible for the murders in a range battle known as the Spring Creek Raid.

Alston was the first warden to be appointed by the state of Wyoming. Previous wardens were appointed by the lessee of the prison and the mission was to make money using prison labor. After Alston took office in 1911, he set about to reform penitentiary conditions. He brought books into the system, helped educate the inmates, and added a regimen of physical fitness and recreational activities, including football, track, and baseball. He was credited with transforming the prison from a harsh penitentiary to a house of corrections.

Felix Alston believed baseball to be a great source of inspiration—a sport that makes everyone who plays necessary to somebody else.

An avid fan of the Detroit Tigers, and Ty Cobb in particular, the warden sought to form a ball club that would rival any major league outfit. Working with a few choice guards and loyal prison staff members, Alston recruited the fastest and most talented players from a pool of death row inmates. Reasoning, in the beginning at least, that these men appreciated the chance to play more than the average prisoner.

The inmates began playing baseball in February 1911, and they quickly became a cohesive unit. By the end of March the team was playing like a well oiled machine. The hitting, pitching, and fielding talent was as diversified as the crimes each had committed. It wasn't until Alston arrived on the scene, however, that they became an officially organized team and began playing games against other teams in the area.

Alston watched with pride as the prisoners took their positions on the field and played with the grace and force he'd hoped for. At local saloons he bragged that all his players were stars that could beat any team in the territory. The captain of the Rustlers, one of the best clubs in Rawlins, took offense to Alston's claim and challenged his "All Stars" to a game. When Alston balked the Rustlers' captain sweetened the contest with a $50 wager. The warden accepted.

It was a brisk spring afternoon when the All Stars and the Rustlers met at the city park to square off. News of the game had spread through town and residents came to see the men play.

Armed guards ushered the prisoners onto the field. The 11 member team was chained together and lined up in front of the dugout. Alston eyed his players from the stands, surrounded by reporters from the *Rawlins Daily Times* newspaper.

Three guards unlocked the irons binding the team and they scurried off to their positions. A battery of other guards leveled their weapons at the men and fanned out around the field. The All Stars tossed a ball back and forth from base to base to outfield. Each player aggressively and accurately scooped up every ball that came their way. Alston smiled proudly as he ran down the roster of players for the reporters:

"Leroy Cooke is at first. He bludgeoned to death a barber and stole his money. On second base is George Saban. He shot his wife and two children. Jack Carter, third base. Shot and killed an old hermit, cut him up and burned his remains in the fireplace. Benjamin Owen, beat his neighbor to death with a hatchet. Horace Donavan, catcher. Shot and killed his brother-in-law. Fielders Simon Kensler, Darius Rowan and Lazlo Korda—between them they raped and killed eight people. William Boyer, pitcher. Stabbed his father to death with a letter opener."

The reporters jotted the information down, a little taken aback by the violent past of the men on the field. One of the writers looked away from his pad and watched a short, well-built man with a thick mustache eagerly snap up every ground ball that came his way. The player hurled the ball to first with a rocket arm.

"Who's the short-stop," the reporter inquires. Alston took a moment to admire the ball player's form before he responded. "Joseph Seng," he answered. "He's the newest member of the team."

"What did he do?" the reporter asked.

"He unloaded a revolver into a man's head," Alston answered.

The All Stars lost their first game by one run. The warden was disappointed, but determined to work the team harder. He believed they had championship potential, but simply lacked the necessary motivation to win.

Back inside the prison, Alston decided the best incentive he could give the All Stars to win their next game would be their life.

At the next practice he announced to the inmates that as long as the team won each challenge he would arrange for their stays of execution. Anyone not playing at their best would be removed from the team and his execution expedited.

Alston was confident the men would do whatever it took to avoid the gallows.

Felix Alston was warden of the Wyoming State Penitentiary for eight years, from April 17, 1911 to March 1, 1919, and was the driving force behind the prison baseball team's hustle. He had previously been the Big Horn County Sheriff in northern Wyoming. (Photograph courtesy of the Wyoming State Archives Dept.)

Wyoming State Penitentiary All Stars team photo—Joseph Seng is seated second from left. The players are individually profiled in the following pages. As in the cover photograph, the warden's son, Felix Jr., is seated in the center as the team mascot. (Photograph courtesy of the Wyoming State Archives Dept.)

Warden Alston was a huge fan of major league baseball star Ty Cobb, and encouraged his players to emulate Cobb's style and technique. This image shows the cover to the sheet music for "King of Clubs," a song by William Brede that was published in 1912. The song was dedicated to Ty Cobb, who played for the Detroit Tigers and won batting titles in the three previous years, 1909, 1910, and 1911.

Name: Leroy C. Cooke
Position: 1st Base
Alias: None
Crime: 1st Degree Murder
Age: 23
Weight: 170
Born: 1888, Missouri
Occupation: Ranch Hand
Sentence: Death

Teammates said he was "a brain wrapped in sandpaper." He knew almost every answer connected with baseball.

Name: Lazlo Korda
Position: Left Field
Alias: None
Crime: Murder/Rape
Age: 27
Born: 1885, New York
Occupation: Rail Yard Worker
Sentence: Death

A scrapper, banty rooster who'd fight at the drop of a hat, Korda's teammates said he'd "get into fights and hit so fast they couldn't see his hands move."

Name: George Saban
Position: 2nd Base
Alias: Captain
Crime: Murder
Age: 31
Weight: 180
Born: 1880, Wyoming
Occupation: Rancher
Sentence: Death
A great batsman and superior fielder, Saban would bet on anything, including his own team.
(Photograph courtesy of the Wyoming State Archives Dept.)

Name: Jack Carter
Position: 3rd Base
Alias: None
Crime: Murder
Age: 25
Weight: 177
Born: 1886
Occupation: Bartender
Sentence: Death
"If I had to do over again I'd still been a crook, but I would have fought harder to get on the All Star team sooner."—Jack Carter, 1910.

Name: Benjamin Owen
Position: Pitcher
Alias: Benji O.
Crime: Murder
Age: 37
Weight: 183
Born: 1874, Wyoming
Occupation: Laborer
Sentence: Death

Teammates said he had a true bullet arm, but was "afraid of his own shadow, sobbed time and time again over his impending death."

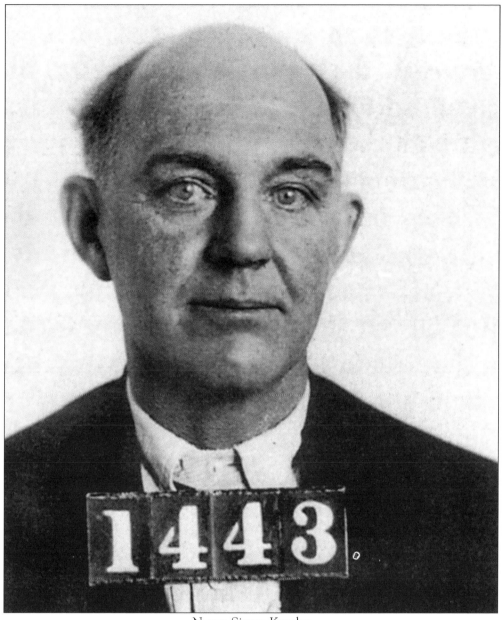

Name: Simon Kensler
Position: Right Field
Alias: None
Crime: Murder/Rape
Age: 38
Weight: 178
Born: 1873, Pennsylvania
Occupation: Laborer
Sentence: Death
Oldest member of the All Stars, Kensler was the kind of guy his teammates
wished was their uncle.

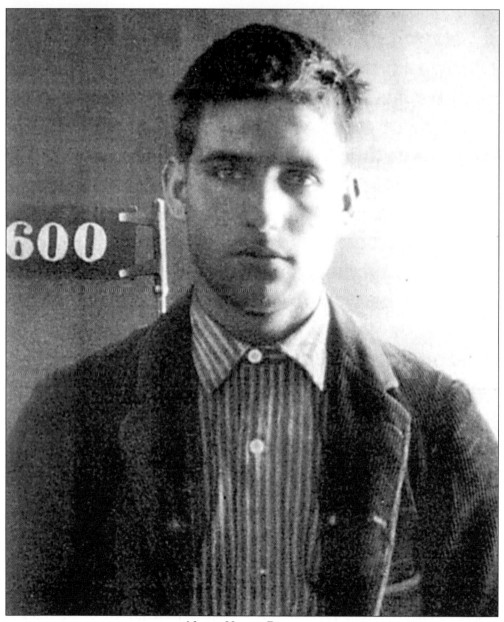

Name: Horace Donavan
Position: Catcher
Alias: None
Crime: Murder
Age: 19
Weight: 172
Born: 1892
Occupation: Rail Yard Worker
Sentence: Death
He had a toughie's chiseled chin and steely eyes. He was the youngest player on the All Star team and the most popular with teenage girls.

Name: Darius Rowan
Position: Center Field
Alias: Ro
Crime: Murder/Rape
Age: 29
Weight: 192
Born: 1882, Alabama
Occupation: Laborer
Sentence: Death

Rowan had a powerful body and was an agile, eagle-eyed player who struggled with a speech impediment and was unable to read.

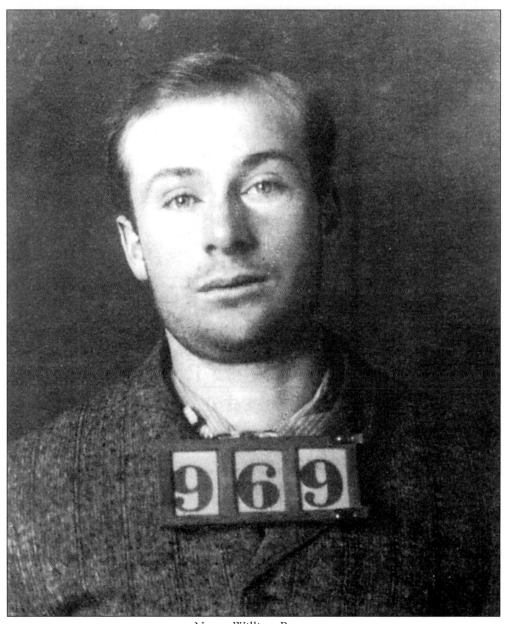

Name: William Boyer
Position: Pitcher
Alias: None
Crime: Patricide
Age: 25
Weight: 182
Born: 1887, Wyoming
Occupation: Rail-Yard Worker
Sentence: Death
"No on ever thought I'd amount to anything. At the hotel I managed to prove 'em all wrong."—William Boyer, 1912

Name: Joseph Seng
Position: outfield and shortstop
Alias: none
Crime: murder
Age: 29
Weight: 152
Born: 1883, Allentown, Pennsylvania
Sentence: Death
"I desire to thank all those people of Rawlins who have taken such an interest in my welfare and for the kindness extended to me by them."
—Joseph Seng, May 2, 1912, just weeks before he was hanged.
(Photograph courtesy of the Wyoming State Archives Dept.)

This is a 1911 drawing of the All Star team, made by one of the residents of the Crossbar Hotel.

This is the mess hall of the Crossbar Hotel as it looks today as part of the Wyoming Frontier Prison Museum. It probably did not look so clean in the early 20th century when it was in use as a prison.

THREE

Betting on a Win

A short, wiry pitcher throws left-handed with pinpoint accuracy, delivering a third strike to the eager batter at the plate. The umpire loudly announces that the player is out and the catcher whips the ball back to the mound. The indignant batter curses at the umpire and flips his bat carelessly over his shoulder. Outraged at the poor sportsman like behavior the arbitrator ejects the player from the game. In an instant the umpire is flat on his back in the dirt and the disgruntled batter is punching him hard in the mouth. The player repeatedly kicks the umpire, knocking out his teeth and breaking his ribs. The batter is eventually subdued by opposing team members and ushered off the field. The unconscious umpire is then rushed by ambulance to a nearby hospital.

Baseball fans expecting to see such a scene would not find it any of the games in which the Wyoming State Penitentiary All Stars played. However, the uncivilized behavior of "baiting" an umpire could be found in the major leagues. The practice escalated in 1911 when Philadelphia A's manager Horace Fogel encouraged his team to physically challenge umpire's calls.

A's left fielder Sherry Magee took Fogel's suggestion to heart when he beat umpire Bill Finneran to a pulp. He was suspended for the season and fined $200 dollars. Fogel stood by Magee's actions saying it was necessary to send a message to all umpires that "bad calls would not be tolerated."

In the 1911 season, Cincinnati Reds center fielder Bob Bescher set a National League record with 81 stolen bases, pitcher Rube Marquard topped the league with 237 strikeouts, and Ty Cobb hit for a career best .420 average. All Star manager Felix Alston pushed his team to play like the major league stars making headlines, but drew the line at unruly behavior.

Alston was not only influenced by the talent he saw in the major leagues, but was fascinated by the marketing skills and superstitions of teams such as the Philadelphia A's. Many teams hired cripples, dwarfs, or zany illiterates to serve as mascots, believing they would bring good luck. Louis Van Zeldt, an undersized hunchback, was the A's mascot and was credited with helping them to win the World Series. Taking a cue from the game's best, the warden enlisted his four-year-old son to be the All Star's mascot.

Emulating professional teams light-hearted quirks and outstanding play was not the only aspect of the sport Alston chose to adopt. Gambling on games was also mimicked.

The practice of betting on various ball clubs began almost as soon as Abner Doubleday mythically laid out the rules for the game. Placing and collecting bets on games was a common practice. Gamblers coast to coast were making a fortune buying up one or more players to lose a game and then wager they would do so. To many sport's columnists, it seemed at times that morals were so low that you couldn't witness a game between many of the clubs and be sure that both sides were striving to win. The struggle between baseball and those who would corrupt it was present in Wyoming as well.

Three state politicians raised money for their reelection campaigns betting on the All Stars to win. Eleven Carbon County businessmen increased their bank accounts backing the inmate players. And many Rawlins residences cashed in on All Star victories laying hard earned dollars on the team.

During their 1911–1912 season, the Wyoming State Penitentiary All Stars played 45 games and had a 39-6 record. It is estimated that more than $132,000 dollars in bets exchanged hands in the county.

According to territory historian Lowell Evers, "everyone was making a profit off the inmates."

Warden Alston's incentive for the prisoners to win proved profitable for many, but not everyone was pleased with their performance. A rival team, the Fighting Juniors, were the best team in the region until the All Stars arrived on the scene, and the Junior's sponsor was not happy they could lose their reputation as the best team to a bunch of death row criminals. Valentine Wood, Jr., the owner of Junior's Plumbing Supplies, sent scouts to monitor the All Stars' games and identify the weakest link. Once the team's vulnerabilities were discovered, Wood ordered his players to concentrate their efforts on that area. For Wood, remaining the better team outweighed the revenue being made off the All Stars. He vowed to find a way to bring down Alston's team.

Although small in number, some Rawlins citizens took exception to the rampant territory-wide obsession with baseball. They further believed the added pressure placed on the prisoners to win was barbaric.

In the early twentieth century betting on baseball continued to be a growing problem throughout the country. Repeated attempts were made to fix the World Series and many key players were persuaded to toss regular season games.

In 1911, rumors were abounding that gambling had contaminated the most popular pitcher in the major leagues. Christy Mathewson, the Philadelphia A's star pitcher, had sat out the World Series in 1905. Team officials and coaches reported that he had "hurt his shoulder romping around with his teammates aboard the train." The year the All Stars took the field, a handful of former professional players were claiming gamblers had promised to make it worth Mathewson's while if he sat out a game or two

The Wyoming State Penitentiary All Stars square off against the Cheyenne Indians in Cheyenne, Wyoming, in 1912.

The prison warden, Felix Alston, had this framed photograph of the World Champion Philadelphia A's over his desk in his prison office. The Philadelphia Athletics won the world series in 1910, 1911, and 1913 under the leadership of manager Connie Mack and the play of hall of fame second baseman Eddie Collins. Mack was the longest serving manager in baseball history, leading the Athletics from 1901 all the way through 1950. They also won world series titles in 1929 and 1930.

Warden Alston continued to enjoy baseball even after the All Stars were no more. The lobby card for the 1913 short film *Breaking into the Big League,* featuring Christy Mathewson, was among the items found in Warden Alston's office.

This studio photograph of Warden Felix Alston's children was probably taken in Basin, Wyoming (circa 1910), while he was sheriff. The children are (left to right) Mayne Virginia, age 8; Helen Lila, age 4; Felix, Jr., age 5; and Eunice, age 10. As adults the children all claimed Rawlins, their hometown.

OUR WARDEN
Felix Alston

PROGRAM
WYOMING STATE
PRISON SHOW
DECEMBER 25TH
1915

THE WYOMING PEN

Assorted Prison Publications circa 1912.

Every Hour During the Day

thousands of homes business houses, etc. are being kept "spick and span" with RUG-BEE and TRY-ME BROOMS

Sold Everywhere

Laramie Broom Works, Manufacturers

Quality First

General Offices: Ogden, Utah

AN ORIGINAL MELO DRAMA IN THREE ACTS

ENTITLED

"The Fatal Bonanza"
(By F. L. Boyd)
(Scenery painted and arranged by J. Warne

CAST OF CHARACTERS

Richard Bland, a miner . . . . . F. L. B
Kitty Bland, his daughter . . . O. Harr
Fanny, Bland's wife . . . . Dick Hender
Dudley Hawkins, rancher . A. Guy Hawk

J-A-B-S

Vol. I   No. VIII
$1.20 the   10c the
Year   Copy

JULY, 1916

Edited and Published Monthly by
Inmates of Wyoming State Prison at Rawlins, Wyoming

YOU CERTAINLY "AUTO" WEAR
one of my genuine hand-made horse-hair

Belts and Hat-bands

Mr. Good Dresser
They are not too "loud," just right.
Horse Hair and Leather Bridles & Quirt
Ladies' Beaded Hand-Bags
and Opera Shawls
Fancy Whisk Brooms

GOODBYE

BE IT KNOWN that after this issue J-A-B-S will change its name to "The Underworld;" the new magazine will be under the efficient guidance of Editor Gorman and his staff, who have the ability to produce a far better magazine than J-A-B-S. All unexpired subscriptions will be filled by "The Underworld."

A caricature of Felix Alston is seen here in a page of the prison magazine. The magazine was just one of several reforming methods Alston put into place once he was made warden. The drawing was made by a prisoner at the penitentiary.

The Cheyenne Indians team, pictured here, was one of many western teams the All Stars competed against regularly. (Photograph courtesy of the Wyoming State Penitentiary Archives Dept.)

One of the Rawlins' early baseball teams that challenged the All Stars. Many of these men were fans of Joseph Seng.

THE "HOUSE" BASEBALL TEAM.

The Oregon State Penitentiary baseball team would have been worthy opponents for the All Stars if they had been granted permission to play against the Wyoming State Penitentiary club. Fearing his prisoners would chance a massive escape, the Oregon Prison warden would not allow the teams to meet

Valentine Wood, Jr. was owner/manager of Junior's Plumbing Supplies and Warden Alston's chief nemesis.

Valentine Wood's passion was baseball, and he wanted more than anything to retain his team's championship status. To that end, he devoted a great deal of time recruiting and working with preteen players, training them for a position with his club when they were of age. A group of Wood's young ballplayers is seen here.

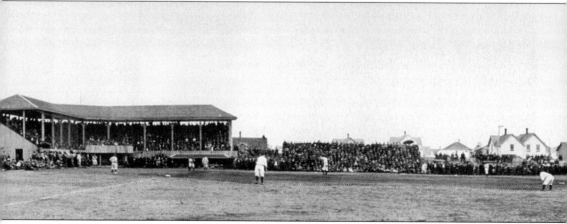

The Wyoming Plumbing Supply Company Juniors warm up on the field before facing their fiercest competitors.

The Juniors pose for a team photograph after practice.

Pitcher Gavin Stanwood was the Fighting Juniors' most valuable player.

BALL AT PEN.

That was an interesting game of ball at the pen Sunday morning between the Junoirs and the penitentiary team although the Juniors were clearly outclassed.

The Juniors were the first up to bat and Bradv fanned out. The Juniors could not get a hit and failed to reach first. Magor let the first convict walk but he was thrown out at second, They got men on second and third but were retired before they made a run.

The Juniors did better in the second getting one run home. Seng was put out going to first and then Fitzgerald knocked a three base hit that scored a run.

The next inning was a shut out for the Juniors, Magor getting as far as third before the side was retired. The same thing happened to the convicts, no runs being made on either side in this inning

Wallace of the Juniors made a run after two men were out in the fourth inning and the convicts got two runs.

OMelia made the star hit for the Juniors getting a home run in the fifth inning but the bases were empty and the best he could do was to tie the score. The convicts didn't want it tied and put two men over the home

This article, entitled "Ball at Pen," so enraged Valentine Wood that he beat the dugout on his practice field with a bat, and kept at it until the roof was completely smashed. The Juniors played hard, but the All Stars were a tough team to beat.

Warden Alston wanted his pitchers to throw like Christy Mathewson, believing his arm was the best in the major leagues. Mathewson, a hall of fame star for the New York Giants, won 373 games in his career, tying him for third all-time. He led the Giants to the World Series four times, including three against Connie Mack's Philadelphia A's. The Giants beat the A's in 1905—when Mathewson amazingly threw three complete game shutouts—but lost to them in 1911 and 1913.

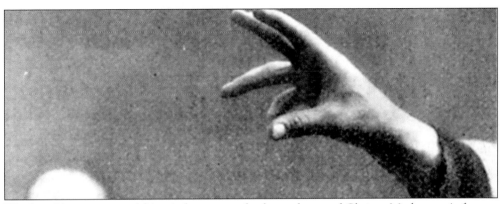

Warden Alston pressured his pitchers to study these photos of Christy Mathewson's famous pitching techniques, in hopes that they could duplicate Mathewson's success.

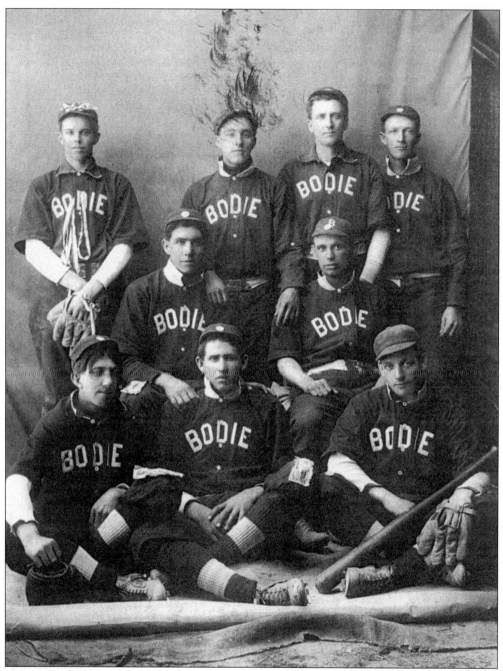

The Bodie Bandits of Bodie, California traveled more than 900 miles to meet the Wyoming State Penitentiary All Stars on the field of battle. For their efforts, the All Stars gave them a game they'd never forget—soundly beating the Bandits 13 to 5.

A hopeful team from Laramie warms up in preparation for their first game of the season against the Wyoming State Penitentiary All Stars in 1911.

Rawlins' citizens were true baseball fans and would roll out the red carpet whenever a game was in town. Hanging over the main thoroughfare in downtown Rawlins in 1911 is a hand-painted sign proudly announcing the big event.

The Carbon County Volunteer Band kept fans entertained between innings during the games with their lively rendition of "Take Me Out to the Ball Game" and a tribute to the home town favorite All Stars with an original piece entitled "Redemption on the Diamond":

Redemption on the Diamond

Hooray for their pride and each day they survive
To make up for their crimes and not yield
With mighty hits and throws the All Star players go
To make right their wicked plight on the field.

FOUR
The Big Hitter

Joseph Seng, a textile worker from Pennsylvania, took a long drag off the butt of a cigarette and blew smoke rings into the air. For the thousandth time he took in his surroundings—an five-by-seven brick room with a heavy iron barred door serving as the only access. A small porcelain latrine was stuffed into a corner, as far from his cot as possible. This was death row inmate No. 1612's home within the walls of the Wyoming State Penitentiary. Incarcerated in 1910 for first degree murder and sentenced to be hanged, the 29-year-old Seng would spend his final days at the Crossbar Hotel.

While awaiting his appeal and execution, his time in jail was spent working in the dispensary and playing baseball. He was the All Stars most valuable player, a right fielder with a rocket arm and a powerful swing. Had he not been so prone to a life of crime he could have played major league ball or pursued a career in medicine, a skill in which he had a natural aptitude.

Born in April of 1882 to German emigrants, Seng was one of 11 brothers and sisters raised in Allentown. After graduating from a Catholic high school, he learned the trade of ribbon weaver and moved to New York. After a short stay in the Big Apple he decided to drift. He traveled from state to state working odd jobs, ending up in Evanston, Wyoming in 1908. There he took a position with the Union Pacific Railroad as a watchman.

His volatile temper and ill treatment of the transients who hung around the rail yard landed him in trouble with his employer on several occasions. William Lloyd, Seng's immediate supervisor, publicly reprimanded him for beating and stealing from the hobos. Seng was outraged at being castigated in front of his co-workers and the two men quarreled. Lloyd fired the hot-headed Seng. Seng insisted the firing had more to do with an ongoing dispute the two men were having over a woman than with problems on the job. He threatened Lloyd's life, vowing Lloyd would end in jail for his actions or in his grave.

Days after Seng's dismissal, he shot and killed William Lloyd. With Lloyd's wife looking helplessly on, Seng fired a .41 caliber Colt revolver into the man's head. While Lloyd was still on the ground, Seng shot him two more times in the skull.

Throughout the trial, Seng maintained that Lloyd was planning to kill him and that he simply "beat him to it."

The jury refused the argument and after deliberating for three days, they found him guilty. Seng appeared indifferent to the serious situation and before being led out of the courtroom, he half smiled and nodded to his attorney. His cocky attitude was instantly checked by the no nonsense guards at the Wyoming State Penitentiary.

Although Seng had been in and out of trouble since he was a teenager this was the first time he had been sentenced to such a strict facility. Once he put on his prison garb the gravity of his plight sunk into his brain. This was his last stop before the cemetery.

As he sat on his cot, smoking and admiring his bawdy baseball card collection, which one of his brothers had sent him, he remembered the day he tried out for the All Stars. George Saban, inmate No. 1441 and the captain of the team, gave Seng a tryout shortly after he arrived at the Crossbar Hotel.

Seng sat up in the batter's box like a pro and hit the second ball pitched to him, sending a high, vicious line drive over the center fielder's head and into the third story window of the guard's quarters. Seng turned out to be the consistent hitter the All Stars needed.

Warden Alston was inspired by Seng's exceptional ball playing skills and had cleared a place on the mantle in his office for the championship trophy he was sure he'd win. The All Star team consisted of ten quality players, but Seng was the best overall. He was a switch-hitter who could play as well in the infield as the outfield.

Ticket buyers lined up for blocks for a chance to see Joseph Seng throw a player out at first or hit a home run. He was the Wild West's version of Shoeless Joe Jackson. Idealistic young boys in the stand would chant Seng's name as he took his place on the field. After a game they rushed the dugout, pen and paper in hand, hoping to get his autograph.

Seng wasn't the only felon with a following. Pitcher William Boyer and catcher Horace Donavan were crowd pleasers too. Donavan excelled at stealing bases and Boyer was a left handed thrower with a wicked knuckle ball. No matter how good the other team members were, fellow inmates insisted Seng was the most valuable player. Team captain George Saban claimed he was the best and most versatile player he'd ever seen.

The positive influence of baseball and months on death row transformed Seng's once arrogant attitude to humility.

His improved temperament led state penal officials to authorize his employment in the prison dispensary. He was made a nurse and helped care for fellow inmates, which included Alston's All Stars. When a mysterious outbreak of ptomaine poisoning threatened the lives of the entire baseball team, it was Seng's quick treatment that saved them.

Prior to Seng's incarceration at the Wyoming State Penitentiary he had lived recklessly, committing felonies that ranged from drunk and disorderly conduct to robbery. It wasn't until he began serving time on death row that he began living a productive life. It was an irony that was not lost on the convict and one he addressed before his hanging.

I desire to thank all those people of Rawlins who have taken such an interest in my welfare and for the kindness extended to me by them. Their acts have proven a source of much comfort to me in my last hours. I also desire to state that since being arrested for the crime for which I am to die, I never received a square deal until brought to the penitentiary. Warden Alston and his guards have in every way treated me squarely and to them I express my sincerest thanks.

—Joseph Seng, May 2, 1912

This is 1911 photograph of the Crossbar Hotel. Cell Block A, where Joseph Seng spent the last 13 months of his life, is the left part of the building with the tall windows.

Mrs. William Lloyd, the widow of the man Joseph Seng murdered, witnessed the crime and tried desperately to save her husband's life.

DESCRIPTION OF CONVICT

STATE PENITENTIARY, RAWLINS, WYOMING,

April 18th, 1911----,191--

Miss Rose A. Bird,
Hon. ÁXDXGÓXX

Secretary State Board of Charities and Reform:

The following is a descriptive report of____one State------____Convict delivered at this Penitentiary
_____April 18th, 1911---,191--,_ by Sheriff of Uinta County,Wyoming,- - - - -

Registered number 1612- -

Name Joseph Seng- -

Where Convicted and Sentenced Evanston, Uinta County Wyoming,- - - - - - - - - -

County of Uinta- - - - - - - - _ Term of Court _April 1911- - - - - - - - - -

Date of Sentence April 13th, 1911 -

Length of Sentence Death- -

Place of Confinement—Wyoming State Penitentiary, Rawlins, Wyoming.

Crime _First degree murder- -

Sex _____Male------_ Age 20 years- - - - - - -, Nativity_Pa.- - - - - - -

Occupation Ribbon Weaver- - - -, Height 5ft 5in _____, Weight 132- - - - -_ lbs.

Color_____White- - - - - - - - - - - -_ Complexion Medium- - - - - - - - - - -

Hair _Dark chestnut blond- - - - - -_, Eyes _Blue- - - - - - - - - - - - - - -

Has Wife_____No- - - - - - -_, Parents Yes_____, Children No- - - - - - -

Religion_ Catholic- - - - - - - - - -_, Habits of Life Moderately temperate- - - - -

Education__ Common School- - - -_, Relation's Address_ Mother and Father

_____Anthony and Anna Seng, 537 Elleger St. Allentown, Pa.

_____Sister, Mrs. Agness E.Fisher, same address

Marks, Scars and General Remarks____ tat, of American shield and eagle,and scrip

_____U-N-I-O-N- on left fore-arm, Spot scar above wrist left

_____Tatoo of butterfly and hand of cards,four aces ,and pair of dice

_____on right fore arm

_____Large spot scar on right knee

Respectfully,

C. B. Glunz
Warden State Penitentiary.

Among Joseph Seng's possessions left behind at the prison was a series of baseball postcards, including this one that was tucked into the cracked plaster surrounding the sink in his cell.

A BALK

These cards, along with a few other baseball related items, some sent in by fans, some by his brother, were what made up the décor of Seng's cell. Unable to ever attend a professional baseball game, Seng lived vicariously through these colorful cards that were sent to him.

This card, the one above, and the one on the next page, all part of Seng's collection, are rather tame by today's standards, but they were considered quite bawdy at the time.

Covering left field

The Squeeze Play

Joseph Seng is seen here as a young man in Pennsylvania practicing his baseball skills.

Seng's carefree young days were a far cry from life at the Wyoming State Penitentiary. A row of cells is seen here as it looks today. Among the events they hold at the prison museum is a lock down, where you can pay to have a mug shot taken, eat dinner in the prison cafeteria, enjoy a tour of the prison, and then spend midnight to 6 a.m. locked in a five by seven foot cell. (Photograph courtesy of the Wyoming State Penitentiary.)

This stark prison yard was where Joseph Seng and the other All Stars practiced their game.

All Star pitcher William Boyer (left) and catcher Horace Donavan formed a considerable battery for All Star opponents.

This is one of Rawlins' early baseball teams that challenged the All Stars. Many of these men were fans of Joseph Seng. In the early 20th century it was quite common for towns the size of Rawlins to have one or more competitive baseball teams. Today Rawlins has a population of about 8,500. In 1910, all of Carbon County, where Rawlins is located, had a population of about 11,000.

FIVE

The All Stars and the Juniors

A large, excited crowd filled the Rawlin's City Park and more people lined the street outside the grandstands waiting to get in. Honking autos passing by added to the clamor. Union Pacific Railroad owners who lived in Rawlins owned eight of the automobiles in town. On game days they would load them up with All Star fans and take off for the field. It created quite a bit of noise, according to historian Lowell Evers. It was a perfect, sunny day for a ball game and the field that lay out before the spectators was mathematically precise. Very soon the mighty Wyoming Plumbing Supply Juniors, a team that had been making headlines on sport's pages throughout the state, would meet the much talked about All Stars on the manicured diamond. It was a match-up not to be missed.

From their lair near the press boxes the Juniors trotted out and were welcomed with shouts and yells from their supporters and a chorus of the song, "Let's Get the Umpire's Goat." All Star fans went as wild as Juniors' fans. As the prison guards led the team into the dugout the crowd cheered and tossed their hats in the air.

Once the Juniors finished warming up, they hustled back to the shade of their pen to wait for game time. The inmates then took the team's place around the diamond.

Mesmerized youngsters abandoned their spot in line at hotdog and lemonade stands to watch the men toss the ball back and forth. Their seemingly effortless hustle was the envy of every boy studying their play. The All Stars finished their warm up, returned to the dugout, and waited for the official to start things off. "Batters for today's game . . ." the official began, ". . . for the Juniors, Stanwood pitching and Cox catching. For the All Stars, Boyer pitching, Donavan catching."

The voice of the fat little man in the blue suit of an umpire resonated across the diamond to those sitting in the packed grandstands. When he finished the announcement, an untranslatable but never-the-less distinguishable echo rebounded from the hills in back of the park. The umpire strutted back from the center of the diamond toward the backstop, stopping to give home plate a brush with his little broom. Then, straightening up, he yelled in an equally loud voice, "Play ball!"

The rivalry between the two teams had intensified as the season progressed, culminating in one big game to see who would claim supremacy. Bookmakers who suspected Valentine Wood, Jr. was behind the ptomaine poisoning of the inmates, a few days prior to this game, had the Juniors favored to win the big game.

They believed Wood had taken additional measures to ensure a victory. Fans were in store for a fierce battle.

The All Stars, who had been grouped in a huddle around Saban, broke up and dashed onto the field at the umpire's instructions. Joseph Seng was the last All Star to take the field. He walked to his position under a deafening barrage of cheers. "One, two, three!" Seng called out to his teammates. "Let's get em' out of here!"

Neither side scored in the first three innings. In the bottom of the fourth with two men out however, the All Stars broke through with three runs. In their next turn at bat, four more All Stars crossed the plate. When the Juniors failed to score in the sixth, the All Stars once again took charge; with two men down, Seng nearly ripped the cover off the ball as he sent it over the tall wooden wall and out of the ball park.

The Juniors team were becoming increasingly frustrated, causing their play to be riddled with errors. Pitcher Gavin Stanwood succumbed to the pressure, losing control of his pitches. One wild pitch hit All Star third basemen Jack Carter in the head. He instantly dropped to his knees, dazed. The inmates on the bench leapt to their feet and began shouting obscenities and the umpire ordered Jack to take his base. He hustled to first, trying desperately to shake off the effects of the fast ball. It was a great act.

No one suspected anything was wrong. Carter himself didn't realize the extent of his injury at that moment. For his sake and for the sake of the team he pretended to be fine. Once the inning was over he shuffled off the field to the dugout, collecting his glove and hurried to his position. Seng noticed right away that Jack was struggling and encouraged him to sit the inning out. Jack was horrified by the suggestion. "I can't do that," he said fearfully eyeing Warden Alston seated in the dugout. "If it looks like this team can do without me . . . I'm dead." Seng knew Jack was right and reluctantly agreed to cover for him should the need arise.

The second Junior batter to the plate popped a ball up over third. Jack tried to keep an eye on the ball, but lost sight of it at the last minute. Seng pushed past Jack, hurling himself on his stomach with his hands outstretched. Just before the ball hit the ground Seng's glove got under it, and the umpire called the batter out.

A stunned hush fell over the All Stars. From their vantage point it appeared as though Seng had squeezed Jack out of the play. Before the team captain finished chastising Seng for "showing off," Jack broke in and quietly explained the situation to George and the other All Stars.

Warden Alston was never made aware of the reason behind the incident. In his opinion Seng was merely making a spectacle of himself. And for Jack's sake, the team let him believe that.

Finally, with two inning left to play, the Juniors second baseman slapped a single and ran to first, where a pinch runner took his place and later scored.

But the All Stars punched back with 2 more runs in the 8th, plus 1 in the ninth to win 11 to 1. The All Stars advanced to the finals and the Juniors sulked out of the stadium to await the next season. At the conclusion of the game the All Star players had a newfound respect for teammate Joseph Seng. Seng's actions on Jack's behalf proved to his fellow inmates he would look out for them.

It wasn't the first time Seng had dared show a compassionate side. During a game with the Cheyenne Devils earlier in the season he helped save the life of an epileptic player having a seizure. Holding the man down, Seng placed a pen in his mouth and kept him from swallowing his tongue. It was a magnanimous gesture that was much appreciated by the Devils. Seng later confessed to George Saban that his "life in prison had been better lived than on the outside."

The All Stars had one week to prepare for the next game in the race for the championship. The western teams participating in the race had been narrowed down to six. The toughest team on the amateur circuit was the Nevada City Robin Hoods—an ambitious club residing in Northern California. Energized by their recent win, the All Stars believed they could beat the Robin Hoods. They practiced long hours and talked about their chances of "going all the way."

The All Stars never imagined they'd be denied the chance to continue on, but a pair of ambitious reporters from Cheyenne, threatening to expose the practice of granting stays of execution for top ball players, put an abrupt end to the inmates' dreams.

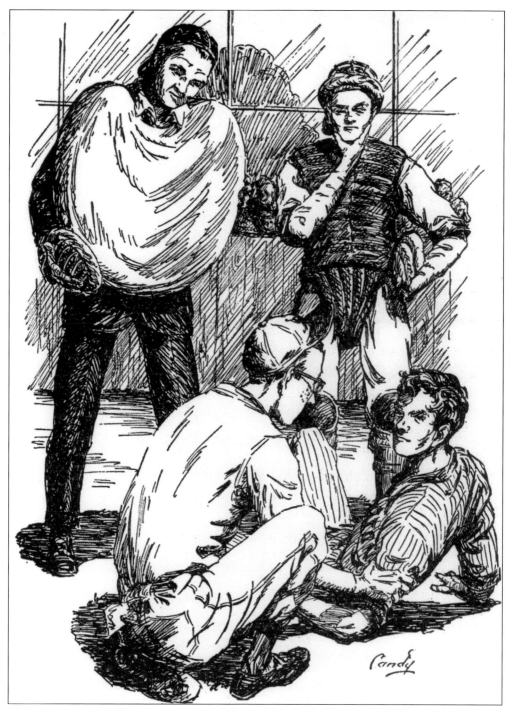

This prison artist's drawing depicts All Star player Jack Carter suffering a fastball hit by pitch in one of their games.

The Klamath County (Oregon) Pirates were a tough ball club that lost to the All Stars both times the teams played.

T. SIGOURNEY, 3d b.   HANLEY, l. f.   A. B. WOLF, Manager.   O'CONNOR, 2d b.   TAYLOR, c. f.
A. MORGAN, 1st b.   ———— COSTELLO, c.   F. MORGAN, l. f.
DeVILBISS, s. s.   W. SIGOURNEY, p.

ROBIN HOOD BASEBALL CLUB.

The Nevada County Robin Hood baseball team, a tough competitor, met the All Stars in Wyoming. Nevada County is in California, just west of Reno, Nevada. Even with today's modern roads, that is over an 800 mile drive. Travel was, of course, much slower in 1911, and the fact that teams would travel such great distances to play a baseball game makes clear the passion that America felt about the game, and why it is called the national pastime.

This was one of the most popular songs All Stars fans sang to baseball officials before and during the games. Written by Nora Bayes and Jack Norworth in 1909, one of the lyrics is "We'll yell, oh you robber! Go somewhere and die. Back to the Bush, you've got mud in your eye." Nora Bayes was a famous vaudeville singer of the time. Today she is best remembered for composing the song "Shine On, Harvest Moon," which was first heard at the Ziegfeld Follies of 1908. Lyricist Jack Norworth is best known for writing the lyrics to the still popular "Take Me Out to the Ball Game" in 1908. The chorus of the song is often sung during the 7th inning stretch of major league games. Few know that there are verses that go with the song as well.

PRISONERS WON AGAIN

Last Sunday Warden Alston permitted his bunch of fast ball tossers to play a game against the Juniors at Overland Park. There was a good sized crowd in attendance an their, was much enthusiastic rooting for both sides.

The Juniors did not play up to their usual standard and in consequence the prisoners captured the game by the score of 15 to 10.

There are a few classy players among the prisoners and they all understood the game.

PRISONERS WILL PLAY AT FAIR GROUNDS

Warden Alston of the penitentiary has informed us that to comply with a general demand to see his fast team of convict ball players play, he has a plan in mind wherein he can take the team down to the fair grounds for a game with the W S Jr. team some Sunday this month.

The Warden asks that all who attend this game go to the grand stand and not to go out on the diamond while the teams are playing and all who attend will observe this rules it may be the only opportunity of ever seeing this team play ball

This was one of the many teams who competed against the All Stars. (Photograph courtesy of the Wyoming State Archives Dept.)

SIX
Off the Field

Warden Alston stared pensively out his office window watching the All Stars practice on the concrete field below. George Saban was at home plate hitting grounders to the infielders. He barked orders at the inmates and excused no errors. "We have to play harder, sharper, more accurately. We can't get rattled," Alston heard him shout. George pops up a ball to the left side of the infield. Seng waves off the men around him, pounds his glove and makes the catch. Seng spots Alston peering down on them like an ancient Roman politician looking down on Christians being fed to the lions.

The warden turned away from the practice, walked over to his cluttered desk and sat down behind it. He wore a sober expression as he shuffled through the urgent telegrams and letters—his eyes settled on a picture of an elderly woman holding a baby. The name Mrs. Anna Seng was scrawled across the bottom of the photograph. The letter attached to it was written with an elegant hand. The Madonna pose and skillfully drafted correspondence were meant to sway the powers that be into commuting Joseph Seng's death sentence.

"Esteemed and Dear Sir: Your Honor will graciously allow the almost despairing mother of Joseph Seng now preparing for death, in jail at Rawlins, to intercede most humbly, for his pardon. I was always hoping that a new trial might at least change the awful sentence. I do not want to criticize justice done in the case. If only I beg your Honor to spare the life of my son, who had certainly received a good education at home. I cannot express in words what I have suffered since I got the awful news, and being able to lend my dear son any pecuniary aid in his trial. I am afraid even to tell my hard working husband anything of the case, as the sad news might kill him and deprive the large family of its only support. I shall ever be grateful to you for any act of benign clemency. I am sure also that my unfortunate son will prove himself, deeply grateful for such an act, and turn a new leaf."

"Hoping and praying that my humble prayer will meet with your kind acceptance. I remain 'Mrs. Anthony Seng.' Yours gratefully forever."

The desperate mother's letter was just one of the many written pleading for the life of Joseph Seng. Letters from fans and other Seng family members were among the glut of correspondence scattered across Alston's desktop.

There was even a petition drawn up and signed by over 350 Rawlins' citizens asking that Seng's life be spared.

Warden Alston was more interested in a telegram he had received from state supreme court Judge Kenneth Farchi than he was receiving pleas to keep Seng from the gallows. Farchi, a native of Rawlins and a member of the bar for 22 years, had a special interest in the All Stars from the beginning. The judge helped assure stays of execution for the team's best players and saw to it that the stays were reversed if the inmates proved a disappointment on the field. As the All Stars popularity increased, newspaper reporters following the tale of the players began investigating the practice of "playing for time." Judge Farchi, who had bet and won thousands of dollars on the All Star games, was in danger of being exposed. His telegram to the warden described the pressure he was under from the victims families (in particular the family of William Lloyd, the man Seng was convicted of killing) to see to it the ball club members' sentences were being carried out.

"I fear the controversy that would be visited upon this office if the death penalties are not played out soon would be catastrophic. Have scheduled an immediate appeal hearing for Joseph Seng."

Alston studied the telegram, then turned his attention to the newspaper headline next to him which read, "Should Felons Be Allowed on the Field." The warden was fully aware of what he had to do. It had been a good run, but it had come to an end. What began as a simple prison athletic program had mushroomed into a profitable money making venture.

Judge Farchi determined that an immediate statement needed to be made to counteract a barrage of criticism the court and prison was experiencing. Because he was the most popular of the All Star players, Farchi moved Joseph Seng's appeal trial to the top of the docket. The Judge believed this act would put an end to questions surrounding gambling on the All Stars.

Alston informed the team that the remainder of the season would be completed using only inmates in general population. Death row inmates whose appeal hearings were scheduled after the season ended could remain on the roster. All the members of the All Star team were visibly shaken by the announcement. In one cool moment their sole purpose for living out another day had been removed and they exchanged glances of shock and disbelief.

Not long after Alston's announcement Joseph Seng's appeal hearing began. Seng's attorney was unable to convince the Supreme Court to commute his client's sentence. Seng would be put to death the following morning.

Joseph Seng spent his last hours alive writing letters to his loved ones and crying over a picture of his mother. His fellow inmates described his mood as quiet and subdued. In an attempt to make his final moments pleasant, a quartet of prisoners sang religious hymns to him. One of the detainees sang "The Holy City" in such a way that it brought tears to the eyes of many of those who were on the row. Father Marcus Long prayed with Seng, listened to his confessions, and comforted him as he wept.

At 2:15 a.m. prison guards came to Seng's cell to escort him to the gallows. Father Long told Seng's forlorn baseball teammates that he was "in a good frame of mind and prepared to meet his maker bravely."

While waiting to be led to the gallows, Joseph Seng worked on this drawing of a stand of sagebrush that grew around the baseball diamond in the prison.

This was the view of the practice field from Warden Alston's office window. He could keep a close eye on his practicing All Stars.

(COPY)

THE STATE OF WYOMING,)
                      ; SS.
    COUNTY OF UINTA.)

                                    IN THE DISTRICT COURT

                                      DISTRICT NO.3.

THE STATE OF WYOMING,   (
              Plaintiff,:
                          :
    -VS-   :   Order Suspending Sentence.
                           :
JOSEPH SENG,   :
              Defendant.

─────────────────

     Now,on this 13th day of April,A.D.1911,the above
named defendant,Joseph Seng,having given notice by his attorney,
R.S.Spence,Esq.,of his intention to appeal said cause to the
Supreme Court,and whereupon the said defendant,by his counsel,
requests the Court to suspend said sentence until the first day
of the next regular term of this Court,in order to enable said
defendant to perfect his appeal by proceedings in error,it is
therefore,considered,ordered,adjudged and decreed by the Court
that the sentence heretofore imposed against the said defendant
for the crime of murder in the first degree,be,and the same
is hereby suspended to and including the first day of the next
regular term of this Court,to-wit:to and including the 4th day
of September, A. D. 1911.

     Done in open Court,this 13th   day of April,A.D.1911.

                              David H. Craig.
                                             Judge.

On the same day, April 13, 1911, that Seng's original execution order was issued, his lawyer
appealed, and won a delay. The case would be considered again by the state Supreme Court
when it reconvened on September 4, 1911.

(COPY)

THE STATE OF WYOMING,)
                  : SS.
   COUNTY OF UINTA.)

                               IN THE DISTRICT COURT,

                                  DISTRICT NO. 3.

THE STATE OF WYOMING,
          Plaintiff,

   -VS-
                            M I T T I M U S.
JOSEPH SENG,
         Defendant.

    Now, on this __thirteenth__ day of April, A.D. 1911, comes
the above named defendant, Joseph Seng, accompanied by his counsel ,
R. O. Spence, Esq., and the prosecution being represented by,
John R. Arnold, County and Prosecuting Attorney, and the said
defendant appearing at this time for judgment and sentence, is
duly informed by the Court of the nature of the information, the
plea, and the verdict, and was asked by the Court if he had any
legal cause to show why the judgment and sentence of the Court
should not be pronounced against him, and no legal cause being
shown why the judgment and sentence of the Court should not be
pronounced against the said defendant, the Court doth now, upon
the verdict and law, adjudge the said defendant guilty of the
crime of murder in the first degree, and doth pronounce sentence
upon the said Joseph Seng, as follows:
    It is therefore, considered, ordered, adjudged and decreed
by the Court, that you, Joseph Seng, be remanded to the custody
of the Sheriff of Uinta County, State of Wyoming, for a period
not to exceed ten days from this date, and that at any time within
ten days from this date you be transported by the Sheriff of Uinta

County, State of Wyoming, to the State Penitentiary of the State of Wyoming, located at or near the City of Rawlins, in said State of Wyoming, and that you there be, by the Warden of the State Penitentiary confined in said Penitentiary until the 22nd day of August, A. D. 1911, and that upon said 22nd day of August, A.D.1911, before the hour of sunrise of said day, you be by the Warden of said Penitentiary, or in case of death or disability, or absence of said Warden, you be, by his deputy, in all respects according to law, then and there be hanged by the neck until you are dead; and to the imposing of which judgment and sentence the defendant now and here excepts.

Done in open Court this ___13th___ day of April, A.D.1911.

___David H. Craig___
Judge.

The State of Wyoming,)
) ss.
  County of Uinta.)

I, John S. Johnston,- - -Clerk of the Third Judicial District within and for said County and in the State aforesaid, do hereby certify the foregoing to be a full, true and complete copy of the ORIGINAL JUDGMENT AND SENTENCE in the case of the State of Wyoming, vs. Joseph Seng the same appearing of record in this Court.

IN TESTIMONY WHEREOF, I have hereunto subscribed my hand and affixed the official seal of said Court, at my office in Evanston, Wyoming, this __15th.__ day of __April,__ A.D. 1911.

___John S. Johnston,___
Clerk Third Judicial District Court.

"SEAL"

This is the court document ordering Seng's transfer to the State Penitentiary at Rawlins, and ordering his execution before sunrise on August 22, 1911.

IN THE SUPREME COURT, STATE OF WYOMING.

Joseph Seng,

   Plaintiff in Error,

    vs.   No. 690.

The State of Wyoming,

    Defendant in Error.

ORDER STAYING EXECUTION.

On this day came the plaintiff in error, Joseph Seng, by his attorney, R.S. Spence, and presented to me an application for a suspension of the execution of the sentence pronounced upon the said Joseph Seng by the District Court of the Third Judicial District of the State of Wyoming, in and for the County of Uinta. And it appearing thereby and from the papers herein filed, that the said Joseph Seng was, at the April, 1911, term of said District Court, convicted in said District Court of the crime of murder in the first degree, and that at said April, 1911, term of said District Court said Joseph Seng was, by said court, sentenced to suffer death by hanging, the execution to occur at the State Penitentiary, as required by law, and that, in and by the said sentence, the date of the execution thereof was fixed for the twenty-second day of August, A.D. 1911. And it further appearing that a petition in error has been filed in the office of the clerk of said Supreme court of Wyoming praying for a reversal of the said judgment and sentence, and that a summons in error has been duly and regularly issued thereon by the clerk of said supreme court. And it further appearing that said Joseph Seng, pursuant to said sentence and the statute in such case made and provided, has been or will soon be taken to and confined in the State Penitentiary to abide said sentence or the further orders of the proper court in the premises.

Now, Therefore, by virtue of the statute in such case made and

provided,and by authority and in pursuance of the command of its
provisions,it is now ordered that the execution of the sentence
aforesaid be, and the same is hereby, suspended until the proceedings
in error herein shall be heard and determined. It is further ordered
that the clerk of said supreme court transmit a certified copy of this
order forthwith to the clerk of the District Court of the County of
Uinta,in said State,and to the Sheriff of that County,and also to
the Warden of the State Penitentiary for their respective information
and direction in the premises.
Done at Chambers this 17th day of July, A. D. 1911.

(Signed) Cyrus Beard
Chief Justice of the Supreme Court
of the State of Wyoming.

The State of Wyoming,)
) ss.
County of Laramie,)

                   I,William H.Kelly,Clerk of the Supreme
Court of the State of Wyoming,do hereby certify that the above and
foregoing is a full,true and correct copy of an order made this day
in the case of Joseph Seng,plaintiff in error, vs. The State of Wyoming,defendant in error,now pending in the Supreme Court.

    Witness my hand,and the seal of said Supreme Court,at Cheyenne,
this 17th day of July, A. D. 1911.

WILLIAM H. KELLY,
Clerk of the Supreme Court.

"SEAL"

Warden Alston was successful in getting Seng's execution delayed long enough that he was able
to play baseball for most of the 1911 season. This July 17th, 1911 document signed by Cyrus
Beard, the Chief Justice of the Wyoming Supreme Court, stays the execution indefinitely;
"suspended until the proceedings in error herein shall be heard and determined."

In the end, Wyoming Governor Wyoming Joseph Carey would not stay the execution of Seng any longer, or commute it to a life in prison sentence. Carey served one term as Wyoming governor, from 1911 to 1915. He started his career working for the campaign of U.S. Grant for the presidency. He was rewarded with being named the U.S. District Attorney for Wyoming, and soon became an associate justice on the Wyoming Supreme Court. He tired of public life and began a successful ranching career with his brother in 1879. Eventually, he was pulled back to public life, becoming mayor of Cheyenne, and then the first U.S. Senator from Wyoming, being elected on November 12, 1890. (Photograph courtesy of the Wyoming State Archives Dept.)

DAY LETTER
THE WESTERN UNION TELEGRAPH COMPANY
INCORPORATED
25,000 OFFICES IN AMERICA   CABLE SERVICE TO ALL THE WORLD

RECEIVED AT 217 W. 17th St., Cheyenne, Wyo.
19. D. Q.   63 BLUE   3 70

                    Allentown, Pa. May 12, 1912   8

Hon. Govenor Jseph M. Carey,

                    Cheyenne, Wyo.

Understanding this is mothers day which you institute in Wyoming
to honor the worthy mothers of the people of your state I appeal to you to relieve my afflictions by commuting the death
sentence of My son to life imprisonment. I pray your
honor to make at least one mother happy and will appreciate
your clemency at the moment of my greatest distriss.
                    Mrs. Anna Seng

1036.A.M.

Anna Seng sent this telegram on May 12, 1912, making a desperate appeal for the life of her son.

To the Honorable the District Court of the Third Judicial District
of the State of Wyoming,Sitting Within and for the County of Uinta,
and to Honorable Felix Alston,Warden of the State Penitentiary of
the State of Wyoming;

GREETING:

WHEREAS,in a certain action which was lately heard in our
Supreme Court,wherein Joseph Seng was plaintiff in error and the
State of Wyoming was defendant in error,the following order,judg-
ment and decree of our said court was made and entered of record in
said Court and cause on the second day of April,A.D.1912,viz:

"Joseph Seng,   )
)
        Plaintiff in Error   )
)
        vs.   )
)
The State of Wyoming,   )
)
        Defendant in Error.)

This cause having been heretofore argued and submitted and taken
under advisement by the Court and the Court being now fully advised
in the premises,doth now hand down and deliver its opinion herein,
which is ordered to be filed in this case;and for reasons set forth
and stated in said opinion it is ordered that the judgement and sentence of the district court herein,to-wit:The District Court of the
Third Judicial District of the State of Wyoming,in and for the county
of Uinta,be,and the same is hereby,in all respects,affirmed;all the
Justices concurring.

And Joseph Seng,the said plaintiff in error herein,having been
convicted in said district court of the crime of murder in the first
degree,and having been sentenced by said court on the 13th day of
April,A.D.1911,to be hung on the 22nd day of August,A.D.1911,and the
execution of said sentence having been suspended by the order of the
Chief Justice of this Court at the time the petition in error

was filed,this Court doth now order and appoint the 24th day of May, A.D. 1912, as the day for the execution of said sentence.

It is therefore ordered that the said sentenced pronounced by the said District Court be in all respects carried out and executed on the said 24th day of May, A. D. 1912.

It is further ordered that a certified copy of this order be trasmitted to the clerk of the District Court of Uinta County, and that a certified copy thereof be also transmitted to the Warden of the State Penitentiary,and that said certified copy transmitted to said warden,together with the warrant issued by the clerk of said district court upon said sentence,shall be said warden's sufficient warrant and authority for executing said sentence and judgment."

State of Wyoming, ⎱
             ⎰ ss.
County of Laramie. ⎰

I,William H.Kelly,Clerk of the Supreme Court of the State of Wyoming,do hereby certify that the above and foregoing is a full, true and correct copy of the order and judgment made on the 2nd day of April, A. D. 1912,in the case of Joseph Seng,plaintiff in error, vs.The State of Wyoming,defendant in error,as the same appears of record in said court.
Witness my hand and seal of said Supreme Court at Cheyenne,Wyoming, this 3rd day of May, A. D. 1912.

William H. Kelly.
Clerk of the Supreme Court of the
State of Wyoming.

"SEAL"

In the end, the stays of execution ran out, and time caught up with Seng. This court document, made on April 2, 1912, calls for Seng's execution on May 24, 1912, and this time the sentence would be carried out, despite numerous last minute appeals from family and fans.

This photo of Joseph Seng's mother, Anna Seng, with her grand-daughter was sent to Warden Alston and Wyoming's Governor Joseph Carey. Seng's mother and brother each sent a copy of the photo. (Photograph courtesy of the Wyoming State Archives Dept.)

16 May 1912

Mrs. Anna Seng,
Allentown, Pa.

Dear Madam:-

Your telegram has been received, and it together
with all of the papers which have come to me have
been filed with the Board of Pardons for their consideration.

Very truly yours,

KT

Joseph M. Carey,
GOVERNOR.

BY

Executive Secretary.

Dictated by Governor Carey
and signed in his absence.

This response from Governor Carey's to Anna Seng concerning her son could not have instilled much hope.

3700

Evansville Ind, May 13th, 1912.

To His Excellency,
Governor Joseph M.Carey,
Cheyenne, Wyoming.
Honorable Sir:-
        I am a boy 23 years old begging you for the life of
my poor brother, whom I love as you love the members of your own
family. A brother to whom I am indebted for a thousand and one
kindnesses- JOSEPH SENG F who is condemned to die on the gallows at
Rawlins Wyoming on May the 24 .
    I do not know what the circumstances are surrounding the crime he
committed, but I cannot believe that our Joe is bad enough for a fate
like that. Governor, he has not a friend between Wyoming and Pennsylvania. Our family is a large one and we all have had to shift for
ourselves. Poor Joe has made his own way since he was a little boy, and
has never been a burden on his mother and father.
    Our people are honorable but we have no means, I am working for
$15. a week and having my expenses to pay out of that I am not able
to save much even to send to my mother at home. So that Joe has not
had a cent to help him in his trouble.
    Joe has never been called vicious; as I knew him he was anything
else. I have not seen him now for six or seven years. Wont you take
into consideration, Governor, that Joe has made his own way since he
was a mere child, with no one to train him, no one to direct him!
Governor, save us this terrible ordeal! We have all had a hard life
We have never known the luxuries, and very few of the comforts, but
our mother and Father have tried,at least, to train us to be honest.
and straightforward. There are sixteen twelve children in our family
and this is THE FIRST CRIME THAT HAS BEEN LAID AT OUR DOOR.
In Gods Name, Governor, save us from this awful blow. Anything but
the gallows as a heritage. we would not even be able to have his body
sent home to Allentown Pa.
    I am enclosing Mothers picture taken with one of her Grandchildren
This is Joe's Mother, Governor, and my mother. She is an upright
Christian woman and this thing will KILL HER! She has raised twelve
children, who are good American citizens. Can you not for her sake
modify the decree that will end her life in disgrace because one of
the flock, who thinking it manly to go out in the world and earn his
own way, has gone wrong?
    Joe is not a degenerate, Governor! I do not know what his crime
is but I would without the knowledge say that it was committed in
the heat of passion or in defense of his life- for Joe (as I knew him)
would not harm a kitten.

      GOVERNOR, IN GODS NAME SAVE US!

        Hopefully, a prostrated brother,

           Frank L Seng

Joseph Seng's younger brother, Frank, wrote this longer, impassioned appeal for his brother's
life to be spared. It was with this letter that the photograph on page 87 was sent. He says there
are 12 children in the family, and this is the first crime laid at their door.

The following three images show personal items left to the prison by Joseph Seng. They were likely sent to him by his fans. This first item is a Honus Wagner baseball card. Wagner, known as The Flying Dutchman, is a hall of fame player considered one of the greatest shortstops in history. He played 21 seasons in the major leagues, mostly for Pittsburgh. In 1909, he led his Pirates to a world series victory over Detroit. The Honus Wagner baseball card of 1909 (not the one pictured here), is the rarest and most valuable baseball card, currently valued at $1.265 million. Being a shortstop himself, Seng likely saw Wagner as a great hero.

The A.J. Reach company was one of the leading manufacturers of sporting goods at the time the All Stars played. The ad asks you to write for their "new 1911 catalogue, printed in color." Reach is perhaps most famous for inventing the cork center baseball, which was eventually adopted by the major leagues around 1927, ending the so-called "dead ball" era, and giving way to home run hitter Babe Ruth, who would revolutionize the game.

This Hal Chase baseball card shows the first star player for the New York Yankees. In his earlier days, he often played second base, something extremely unusual for someone who threw left-handed. With the Yankees he was known as, and is still considered by many baseball historians, as the best defensive first baseman to ever play the game. He left the Yankees in 1913, well before their glory years. His career would end prematurely in scandal, as he was accused of deliberately losing games to keep his team from winning the pennant, and was banned from baseball for life.

SEVEN

The End of the All Stars

Joseph Seng took short sips from the cup of coffee in his hand and smiled as he drank it down. "Cook out did himself with this pot," the condemned man bragged to the visitors in his cell. Father Long and Doctor Maghee, Seng's closest friends inside the Wyoming State Penitentiary, didn't respond. The single cup of coffee Seng was enjoying was his last request before being led to the gallows. When the guards came for him he quickly polished off the final drops of java, bid farewell to the men with him and left the cage. "Tell my mother good-bye for me," he asked the doctor.

The bright moon filtering in through the barred windows cast long shadows of Seng and his escorts on the floor. His legs grew heavier with every step. His face turned pale and his breath came in big gulps. One of the guards turned to him and asked if he was going to make it? "Let's get this over with," Seng told him.

Twenty-five witnesses were waiting in the execution chamber when Seng entered. They wore grim, solemn expressions. Seng was ushered up a flight of stairs and placed in front of a trap door.

He smiled ever so slightly at the onlookers. A black hood was placed over his face, his hands and feet were bound, and the noose fashioned around his neck. The executioner tightened the knot at the base of Seng's left ear—a necessary precaution to ensure a clean break. After a brief pause the executioner instructed the inmate to step forward. Seng faltered a bit, but did as he was told.

The step triggered a chain of mechanical movements. As his weight pressed down the split door, it pulled a cord over a pulley and plucked a plug from a water-filled container at the end of a fulcrum. A metal counter weight hung at the opposite end of its arm. Several long, agonizing seconds ticked by as the water spewed from its metal can onto the ground, finally dropping a counter weight and pulling a cord that jerked the hinged support-pole from beneath the trap where Seng stood. Once the trap's panels dropped, Seng's body free-fell to the end of the rope, snapping like a tip of a whip. He was pronounced dead 9 minutes and 45 seconds later.

In spite of the grief over the loss of their key player, the All Stars managed to gather on the practice field one last time. Seng's absence was keenly felt and his teammates were without the heart for the game they once had.

One by one they left their gloves on the field, abandoning the sport forever.

In the weeks leading up to Seng's execution and the subsequent end of the mighty All Star baseball team in 1912, the prison made newspaper headlines for a deadly incident some Rawlins' residents believed began as a plan to break Seng out of jail.

While guard W.F. Carrick was making his nightly rounds an unknown assailant shot him in the head. According to the Carbon County Journal, it was thought that "someone on the outside had went up to the pen with the intentions of liberating a friend or a relative and had been noticed by the guard before making his way into the yard. A rope ladder and several steel hack saws were found on the prison fence." Carrick had only been working at the penitentiary for three days before he met his death. The culprit responsible for the crime was never apprehended.

Owing to problems within the prison motivated by the All Stars' popularity and loyal following, and the rumors of gambling, baseball would not resume inside the Crossbar Hotel until after World War I. It would be the mid 1920s before penitentiary players would again be allowed to compete against any outside teams.

Five of Seng's teammates followed him to the gallows and five more met their fates in the gas chamber. In December of 1913, All Star team captain George Saban managed to escape from prison and was never recaptured.

Warden Felix Alston retired from his post at the prison in March 1919. He moved to California and spent the remainder of his days fly-fishing on the Kern River.

Wyoming State Penitentiary prisoner Stanley Hudson summed up the problematic final days of Alston's reign over his profitable baseball team and Seng's end in a journal he kept:

Alston was having his troubles. One day he received notice that further trouble lay ahead. The proper authorities forwarded to Alston a warrant which called for the hanging of a prisoner named Seng who had been granted an indefinite stay. The hanging was to take place right away.

Seng was locked in a cell and a death watch placed over him. He was the first man to be hung at the penitentiary. The last man who had been legally hanged up to that time was Tom Horn, hanged at Cheyenne on the 20th of November 1903. They had since passed a law that all hangings take place at the state's prison. Seng was hung on the 24th of May. The shop men were laid off at noon the day before and locked in the cell house.

They built a temporary wall across one corner of the yard which concealed the gallows from view. They secured the same trap mechanism that had been used in the execution of Horn, it had been invented by an old fellow in Cheyenne. Alston had him come down and rig the thing up in working order the day before.

The ball team didn't amount to much after they hanged Seng.

—Stanley Hudson, May 25, 1912

This is the lower half of the penitentiary gallows. These are the same gallows from which lawman turned outlaw Tom Horn was hung in Cheyenne. They had been moved to the State Penitentiary in Rawlins.

A display of the gallows at the Wyoming State Penitentiary Museum demonstrates for visitors how the elaborate system of water weights was used to execute criminals. The museum can be visited online at www.wyomingfrontierprison.com.

NIGHT LETTER

Form 228

THE WESTERN UNION TELEGRAPH COMPANY
INCORPORATED
25,000 OFFICES IN AMERICA   CABLE SERVICE TO ALL THE WORLD

This Company TRANSMITS and DELIVERS messages only on conditions limiting its liability, which have been assented to by the sender of the following Night Letter.
Errors can be guarded against only by repeating a message back to the sending station for comparison, and the Company will not hold itself liable for errors or delay in
mission or delivery of Unrepeated Night Letters, sent at reduced rates, beyond a sum equal to ten times the amount paid for transmission; nor in any case beyond the
ty Dollars, at which, unless otherwise stated below, this message has been valued by the sender thereof, nor in any case where the claim is not presented in writing wi
days after the message is filed with the Company for transmission.
This is an UNREPEATED NIGHT LETTER, and is delivered by request of the sender, under the conditions named above.

BERT C. CLOWRY, PRESIDENT   BELVIDERE BROOKS, GENERAL MANAG

RECEIVED AT 217 W. 17th St., Cheyenne, Wyo.

106 D. O.   57 N. L.   8 Exa.

Rawlins, Wyo., May 11 1912 5/12

Gov. Joseph M. Carey,

      Cheyenne, Wyo.

On behalf of the aged Mother of Joseph Seng any
of them mothers in Rawlins entreat you to grant father
Conrath's plea and on Mother's day to commute the sentence
of Joseph Seng from hanging to life imprisonment petitions signed
by hundred of mothers and fathers in rawlins follow.

        Mrs A. Hayes,
        Mrs Emma Ivy,
        Mrs J. E. Quinn,
                Committee.

           2:40 Am   5/12

This telegram was sent May 11, 1912 by three mothers in Rawlins appealing to the governor to save Joseph Seng and commute his sentence on Mother's Day. The following three pages show samples of the dozen or so pages that accompanied the telegram, filled with signatures by more than 378 Rawlins' citizens, petitioning unsuccessfully to have Seng's life spared. It is clear that his play on the field had won the hearts of the local citizens

To Joseph M.Carey

    Governor of The State of Wyoming.

WHEREAS: There is at present confined within the Wyoming State Penitent
Joseph Seng

iary,a man under sentence to be hanged May 24th 1912 and

Whereas: There are sveral others whose crimes were as great or greater

than his and these men have been commuted to life imprisonment or less,

Whereas:This mans case was not properly presented because he had not

the means to employ proper Counsel and it is generally understood here

that had his case been properly presented his crime would have been

considered manslaughter and not murder and

Whereas: This mans parents are old and feeble and good God fearing and

upright people and there is a large family dependant on them and this

execution would well nigh be a death blow to them and

Wheras:This Man has been of signal service at the Prison and has person

ally saved eleven lives since being confined there and is a Hospital

Nurse and would be of marked service to the State in helping to care for

the unfortunate men in the Prison,

Now THerefore We the undersigned Citizens of the State of Wyoming do

hereby request you as Chief Executive of this State to Commute this man

sentence to Life Imprisonment in place of death.

Signed:

This page and those that follow show some of the hundreds of signatures made by Seng's impassioned fans in an attempt to have his life spared.

L. G. Smith
S. A. Boyce,
" " "
S. W. Reid
C. P. McLane
Dan McPherson
Emma Peterson
Howard Hail
John Burghe
Arthur Girard
James L Holden
C Elmer
Rose Blickfeldt.
Harvey A. Wells
C. Marshall
H Walther.
H. B. Evans
J. A. Davis
M. M. ...
J. W. Allen
Hermann Gall
A. L. Bicksler
Mrs. James Powers
James Powers

Mrs. ...
Mrs Jackson
C Baker
M Squito
Mrs Ed Lafferty
Mrs Ole Larsen
John Mahoney
Mrs Mahoney
Nellie Mahoney
Maggie Mahone
Mrs Conger
Mrs J Ryan
Mrs H McLaughlin
Mrs F D Dennison
Mrs E. C. Dubach
Mrs Jack Johnson
Mrs Pete Carlson.
Ove Blum
Mrs M Graf
Mrs John Hart
Mrs Louis Severson
Mrs S. P. Johnson
Mrs O. J. Johnson
Mrs W. A. McKay.

L E Vivian

C H Conyers

Mrs. C. A. Conyers

Mrs. Dennis Omelia

J H Anderson

Mrs. C. M. Yerpa

Chas B Boyce

Mrs. T. J. Craddock

Mrs. P. C. Merrell

Mrs. B. S. Peet

Mrs. J. E. Hubbard

Mrs. C A Cook

Mrs. R. E. Fowler

Etta M Mumm

Mrs. Amelia Mumm

Sydney Willetts

Rebecca Coukson

Mrs. L. Roy Baker

E E Patrick

Mrs. W. J. Bennett

Mrs. Frank H. Benson

Mrs. L. E. McFarland

Mrs. C J Ehrenfeld

Mrs. Claude Jones

Mrs. C R Bell

Clifford Ivey

Rosa M. Raabe

Mrs. Wm Joyce

Miss Myrtle Ivy

Mrs. H. Blickfeldt

Mrs. H. E. Cohagen

Mrs. A. S. McIntosh

Mrs. H C. Schuffel

Mrs. O. M. Johnson

Mrs. Otto Thompson

Mrs. H. wise

Mrs. Chas Seith

C. A. Clark

Mrs. C. A. Clark

Mrs. M. J. Forbes

Miss Anne Forbes

Mrs. C C Campbell

C C Campbell

Mrs. Thos. O Donnell

Mrs. Jas. Bracken

P. H. Ellis

Mrs. J. Ellis

J. J. Baldwin

Mrs. G. H. Maghee

Mrs. J. Turnislef

This is the State Capitol building where Governor Carey received the letters, petitions, and telegrams begging to have Joseph Seng's life spared.

This is another photo of Governor Carey. He was born in Milton, Delaware on January 19, 1845. His parents were well established farmers and able to provide him with an excellent education. After two years of college, Carey went to the University of Pennsylvania and obtained a law degree in 1867. After campaigning for Grant, Carey spent his career in Wyoming. (Photograph courtesy of the Wyoming State Archives Dept.)

AWLINS. WYOMING.
EYLE & BARBER, PHOT.

Rawlins, Wyoming was a sprawling Western town 6,755 feet above sea level. Seen here in 1912, the railroad dominates the landscape. Today Rawlins is right on Interstate 80, 100 miles west of Laramie.

This is a contemporary view of the inside of the prison. In a five by seven foot cell in a hall like this was where Joseph Seng spent the last year of his life, and when not on the baseball field, this is the scene where he lived out his days, and waited his final hours before being led to the gallows. (Photograph courtesy of the Wyoming State Penitentiary.)

Rawlins, Wyoming, April 28th, 1912.

Hon. Joseph M. Carey,

    Cheyenne, Wyoming.

Dear Governor Carey:-

    I ask your patience and kind consideration of the few words that I address to you in this letter. The keynote of it lies in your proclamation of "Mother's Day", which I received lately and which reads very well.

    The object of my words to you is to ask you to grant a favor on Mother's Day to a mother who I know to be a true mother and worthy of great honor. It is the mother of Joseph Seng, who is sentenced to hang on May 24th. I would feel very guilty in the sight of God if I did not ask this favor of you.

    Mrs. Seng is a mother of the true christian type and a mother of twelve children, of whom her son Joseph proved to be a prodigal. This is no fault of hers and she loves him as a true mother. What good mothers has not experienced the sadness brought on by a boy or girl that has wandered from their parental roof. But who suffers? The mother. She is willing however to bear all except one thing which must crush the life out of her and that is the thought that her son should meet death by the gallows.

    Seng's good people have often written their sad feelings to me.

This is the first two pages of a letter sent by the Reverend Joe Conrath to Governor Carey, asking for mercy for Seng to spare his mother from knowing her son had been hanged. Note

Hon. J. M. C. #2.

They are poor and could give no financial assistance. They have been buoyed up by the one hope that the sentence may be commuted to life imprisonment. The news has been kept from the poor father, less the shock might be the cause of his death. The smaller children know nothing of it. There is one heart that is bearing it all, and that is the heart of a sad mother who pleads to me for mercy for her son. I feel crushed myself at the thought of it. I think to myself "what good is a corpse when life imprisonment is really the supreme punishment?" Death to Seng would be preferable to life imprisonment; Were it not for his poor mother, who will surely die, he says, if he must hang.

Let me plead with you to show your appreciation of a true mother as expressed in your proclamation by using your authority to save Seng from the gallows. What gratitude will come to you from that good mother and family?

Regarding the case itself of Joseph Seng, I wish briefly to state that I have not met a person who is acquainted with the case who is in favor of capital punishment, for the reason that it was not one-sided. Whether Seng is guilty or not of capital punishment is a matter that does not enter into the substance of this letter, as I am asking you this favor in behalf of the good mother who will suffer with her family when Seng shall be a corpse.

I will be very grateful for the kindness you show to this

that Conrath tells the governor that Seng's father and younger siblings don't even know of his life sentence.

1 May 1912

Reverend Joseph Conrath,
Rawlins, Wyoming.

Dear Sir:-

I have your letter of April 28th concerning the
case of Joseph Seng, who was convicted of murder and
is sentenced to be hung on May 24th.

I have not gone into the Seng case as yet, as it
has not been presented to me in any formal way. When
it is I shall certainly give it consideration. Your
letter shall be presented to the Board of Pardons if
the matter comes up for consideration.

                    Very truly yours,

KT

Though written a month after the final court order scheduling Seng's hanging for May 24, this response from Governor Carey to Reverend Conrath makes it sound like he will still look into the case.

16 May 1912

Rev. Joseph Conrath,
Rawlins, Wyoming.

Dear Sir:-

I have the petition recommending the commutation of sentence of Joseph Seng to life imprisonment. I have filed the petition with the Board of Pardons for consideration.

As I understand it, you are the spiritual advisor of Joseph Seng. From the information that we have of the crime and the circumstances attending it I do not see that you can hold out any hope to him. However, I shall further consider the case.

Very truly yours,

KT

Joseph M. Carey,
_____
GOVERNOR.

BY

_____
Executive Secretary.

Dictated by Governor
Carey and signed in his
absence.

Governor Carey's final response to Reverend Conrath, telling the reverend that given the circumstances, he should not hold out any hope to Seng.

POSTAL TELEGRAPH-CABLE COMPANY

NIGHT LETTERGRAM

The Postal Telegraph-Cable Company (Incorporated) transmits and delivers this night lettergram subject to the terms and conditions printed on the back of this blank.

CLARENCE H. MACKAY, PRESIDENT.

RECEIVED AT

DELIVERY, No.

INDEPENDENT   COMPETITIVE   PROGRESSIVE

4—8929   7D lo5 N L 4 Ex

3700

Philadelphia Pa, May 21st, 1912

The Hon Gov.J.M.Carey-Cheyenne, wyo

Honorable Sir;-

        Kneeling in spirit before you most honorable governor,
I be you to spare the Life of my dear and unfortune brother,
Joseph ,and to revoke the sentence of death pronounced upon him.
Be mindful of the tears of his broken hearted mother,have pity of
the anguish of his devoted sister,whose grateful prayers shall
daily be offered up for you and yours,Oh'give my poor Brother
one more chance to live and repent. I ask it again in the name of
him who wills not the death of the sinner,but rather that he
repent and live.

                Sister M.Bonaventura Seng,Franciscian

convent, Glenriddle, Pa 8:45A

This last minute appeal to the governor came from Seng's sister, Sister M. Bonaventura Seng, sent from her convent in Glenriddle, Pennsylvania.

NIGHT LETTER

THE WESTERN UNION TELEGRAPH COMPAN

INCORPORATED

25,000 OFFICES IN AMERICA   CABLE SERVICE TO ALL THE WORLD

RECEIVED AT 217 W. 17th St., Cheyenne, Wyo.

129-D. WS. 29-N.L.

Allentown, Penna., May 20th. 1912.

Governor Joseph M. Carey,

   CHEYENNE, WYO.

Kindly allow me to ask your honor for clemency in the sad case o

Joseph Seng. I humbly ask you in behalf of the poor mother and a

family.

                    Peter Masson,

                         916pm

This is another example of the many appeals to save the life of Joseph Seng.

3200

COPY

25 May 1912

Mrs. Anthony Seng,
Allentown, Pa.

Dear Madam:-

I feel very sorry for you. I am fond of my kind and hope
I always stand ready to favor the right. Unfortunately, your
son went wrong. He died, however, at peace with the world and
with his Maker. After he was convicted he was treated with
every kindness by the warden of the institution in which he
was confined.

Do not get the impression, from anything that has been
said, that he did not have a fair trial; for he did. He was
defended and when the case was reviewed by the Supreme Court
of the state they could find no error in the decision. The
Board of Pardons did not recommend his case as one deserving
of clemency in any way. I wish I could have found justifica-
tion, or even an excuse to avoid the verdict. I could not.

The greatest of all sorrows has come to you, and with all
my heart I regret that it had to be so. It will be my desire
and my hope that time in a measure may assuage your great
grief, and the grief of others to whom Joseph Seng was related
by ties of blood and affection.

Sincerely yours,

KT

Governor Carey's letter of condolence to Seng's mother Anna, written just days after the
execution, expresses compassion and acknowledges her sorrow and loss.

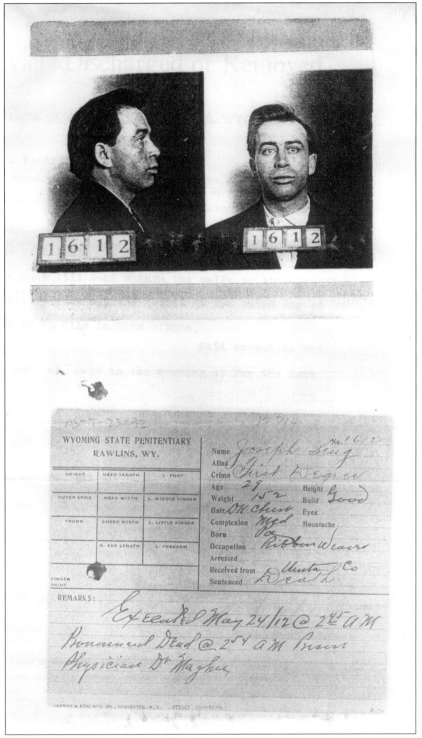

Joseph Seng's death pronouncement, signed by the prison physician, states that he was executed at 2:45 a.m. and pronounced dead at 2:54 a.m.

Convicts Discharged or Removed

STATE PENITENTIARY, RAWLINS, WYOMING

Miss.Mae D.Woodriff.

Secretary State Board of Charities and Reform:

I have to report as follows as to Convict

Joseph.Seng.   *No.* 1612

discharged May the 24th 1912,   *by reason of* death caused by being hung by the neck till dead within the walls of this Institution by reason of mandate of the supreme issued on the third day of April 1912, which is on file in this office.

Said execution was committed at the hour of 2-55 in the morning of May the 24th 1912.

Respectfully,

Warden State Penitentiary.

Note.—This report should be made immediately where any convict is discharged for any reason, or when a death occurs, or any inmates make their escape, with full particulars in each instance.

One can only imagine the thoughts running through Warden Alston's mind as he signed off on the official document removing Seng from the Crossbar Hotel.

Appendix
Checking into the Crossbar Hotel

A cold wind blew flakes of snow through the cracks of the barred windows of the Frontier Prison in Rawlins, Wyoming. Small puddles of melted ice dotted the floor of the aged interior, adding to the frigid temperature hanging in the air. My every footstep echoed off the walls of the empty cells and down the narrow corridors leading to death row. It had been a year since I'd begun researching the notorious western jail, and even with all I knew about its history and occupants nothing prepared me for the desolate setting. Alone in this stark, damp penitentiary I could almost hear the voices of the inmates that did time here—and of those whose lives ended at the gallows.

The baseball field that the popular prison team practiced on was covered with melted snow and the giant stone wall backstop was cracked and chipped. Some of the most ruthless criminals had played ball on the frozen field. Their pitching and hitting had rivaled any major league team in 1911, and their offenses against society rivaled any western renegade of the same time period.

It was that glaring contrast that that first attracted me to the story of the Wyoming State penitentiary All Stars. I happened on to a photo of the prison team while doing research for a book about woman of the Old West. My initial motivation of curiosity quickly grew to an obsession. I devoured all the information I could get my hands on about the penitentiary, the inmates, and the game behind bars. My trip to the actual 100-year-old building itself yielded a wealth of material—artifacts, mementoes, and prisoners' personal belongings were among the items found. Regardless of the controversy surrounding the notion that these hardened criminals were playing baseball for their lives—literally—it was clear to me that the inmates found sanctuary in the sport in the process. They played as though excellence in baseball could redeem their sins.

The following pages are excerpts from the motion picture screenplay about the Wyoming Penitentiary All Stars, their many wins and losses, and one exceptional player named Joseph Seng.

Scene One

FADE IN:

EXT: RAWLINS, WYOMING—AVERILL STADIUM—DAY

A Blinding summer sun pushes its way out from behind a few clouds. The words "Based on a True Story" appear over the golden orb's far reaching rays.

It's a hot July afternoon in 1911. PEOPLE fill the seats of the rickety old arena carved into the center of town. Two teams, the RUSTLERS and the ALL STARS, battle it out on the baseball field below.

An excited ANNOUNCER overseeing the event calls the play-by-play action. It's the bottom of the ninth and the Rustlers are at bat. They're down by two runs and have RUNNERS at first and third.

All Star pitcher BOBBY GUZMAN is on the mound. He eyes the BATTER nervously. There's a lot riding on this pitch. His wind up is full of twists and complicated choreography. He sends the ball sailing towards home plate.
The batter nails the ball hard, knocking out of the stadium. Bobby looks on, stunned. The crowd cheers as the runners race around the bases and tag home.

ANNOUNCER (V.O.): *Amazing! Barrow looked surprised to get a piece of Guzman's fastball. That's the game, folks. The Rustlers take it three to two.*

The loosing team drag themselves off the field and line up single file to shake hands with the opposing team. None of the All Star players say a word.

There's not a trace of satisfaction for a game well played on any of their faces. Each wear a look that's a combination of disappointment and fear.

Bobby is devastated, almost in a daze. His teammates pat his back sympathetically as they pass by him. He forces a smile, but his troubled expression can't be masked.

BOBBY: (to himself) *What have I done?*

The Rustlers head back to their dugout, stopping just before they get there to watch the All Stars line up along the first base line.

Several armed GUARDS approach the All Star players. They hand cuff the men, fix shackles to their ankles and chain them to one another, then slowly usher the team off the field.

ANNOUNCER (V.O): *These state penitentiary players are some of the finest I've ever seen. What a heart they have for the game.*

The Rustlers respectfully applaud and cheer the All Stars as they shuffle towards the exit of the stadium. The crowd follows suit.

The guards lead the inmates to an awaiting bus and the team climbs aboard. Bobby glances back over his shoulder. Tears stand in his eyes as he drinks in the sight of the worn baseball diamond and the fans surrounding it

Scene Two

EXT: WYOMING STATE PENITENTIARY—DAY

A massive, three story building looms against an endless blue sky. High barbed wire fences line the structure on all sides. A weathered plaque on the cornerstone of the entrance reads: Welcome to the Crossbar Hotel.

INT: PENITENTIARY—CONTINUOUS

Warden SHAWN KOSLO stares out a barred window overlooking the prison exercise yard, surveying his kingdom below and grinning.

He wears a crisp, blue suit over his fat, 47-year-old frame. His black shoes are polished and shined to match his hair. He looks like he could piss ice water.

His office door opens and Bobby Guzman enters, flanked on either side by two giant GUARDS. He's carrying his uniform in his arms and he looks pale, almost like he's going to be sick. The guards lead him to a chair in front of Shawn's enormous desk and he takes a seat.

Shawn turns on his heels and slashed a reassuring smile at the despondent player. He plants himself behind his desk and flips open a file sitting in front of him. He studies a copy of Bobby's statistics carefully.

Bobby dabs away the perspiration dripping down his face with the back of his meaty hand. He's a nervous wreck.

SHAWN:
It's not been the best season for you, Guz.

BOBBY:
(stammering)
It . . . it hasn't been that bad.

SHAWN: *Bad enough to lose us the last two games.*

BOBBY: (a little desperate now) *I'll do better.*

SHAWN: *Well, I'm going to have to make some changes.* (pausing, then . . .) *I'm going to need your uniform.*

Bobby struggles a moment to catch his breath. He knew this was coming, but . . . his whole life is flashing before his eyes.

Shawn: *Only the best play.*

Shawn opens up another file, the faint smile leaves his face and is replaced with a hard, serious look. He's God Almighty now, ready to pass out judgment.

BOBBY: (his voice cracking) *I've pitched for you for two years.*

SHAWN: *And I'm grateful. You had a great arm.* (pausing, then . . .) *Your execution will be carried out within the week.*

Bobby is broken. He fights the wave of despair sweeping over him. He reluctantly places the uniform on Shawn's desk and the guards lead him towards the exit.

Bobby does not turn around, he can't. His legs buckle under him as the guards escort him out of the room. Shawn returns to the team statistics on his desk. GEORGE SABAN enters, carrying his faded prison hat in his hands.

George is a Cherokee Indian in his late thirties, with acne-scarred face and a gaunt intensity that's not entirely healthy looking. He's a little nervous, but overall composed. Shawn looks up at George and grins.

SHAWN: *George, do you remember the name of the con who pitched for us the first season we started out.*

George: *Amos Walker.*

SHAWN: *Walker, sure. The ball shot out of his hand like a cannon. Our relief pitcher is as good as he was.*

GEORGE: *Not much of a hitter though and we need a hitter.*

SHAWN: *Well, captain, your job is to get what's needed to win the Western title. It shouldn't be too hard to fid a big stick in here that will play.*

GEORGE: *No, sir. Show me a man that won't participate in baseball and I'll show you a weak, sickly, hot-house plant who'll feel sorry, as he grows older, that he was ever born.*

SHAWN: (half smiling) *I'm counting on you.*

George doesn't return the smile. Shawn's tone was too ominous. He knows any decisions made for the team could mean life or death.

Scene Three

EXT: PRISON—EXERCISE YARD—DAY

JOSEPH SENG stands off by himself in a corner of the stone walled enclosure. His face is bruised and his bottom lip is healing from a cut—all evidence of his run-in with Adams.

He takes a long drag off the butt of a cigarette and flicks it into the grass. In the near distance we see George, PAPPY and CARTER heading towards him from the direction of the baseball field. Carter is carrying a bat.

GEORGE: *Adams was thrown in the hole for a while.*

SENG: (sarcastically) *You want an apology?*

CARTER: *Something like that.*

Seng stiffens up again. His fists clenched at his side.

PAPPY: *George was impressed with the way you took care of business using that club.*

SENG: *I learned how to swing lumber with my father.*

GEORGE: *Did he play baseball?*

SENG: *No. He beat the shit out of me with it.*

GEORGE: *We need hitters.*

CARTER: (with a slight edge) *Now that Adams is out.*

GEORGE: *Can you hit a ball?*

Carter lifts the bat off his shoulder and hands it to Seng. Seng studies the threesome carefully and then takes the stick from Carter.

The men follow Seng as he ambles over to the diamond. Several members of the All Stars are on the field tossing the ball back and forth.

Seng sets up in the batter's box. BOYER, standing on the pitcher's mound, glances over at George. George waves at him to serve up the pitch.

Boyer rockets one to Seng and Seng doesn't flinch. The ball was high and outside. Seng maintains his stance as another bullet sails towards him.

Seng swings as the ball arrives and sends high, vicious line drive over the right fielder's head. The ball sails into the third story window of the guards' quarters.

SMAAAAASHHH!

Glass shatters everywhere.

Pappy and George exchange a delighted look. Seng has made the team.

EXT: PRISON YARD – BASEBALL FIELD – DAY

It's a stifling hot afternoon. The All Stars are in the field. The SPECTATORS in the stands are cheering them on.

The team is up against the MONTANA MAVERICKS. The Mavericks have a RUNNER on second. Owen heads out of the dugout towards the pitcher's mound. Boyer hands him the ball.

The All Stars toss another ball back and forth while the relief pitcher warms up. Cooke tosses the ball to Seng and gives him an encouraging smile.

Seng throws the ball over to Carter. Korda whistles at him from center field.

KORDA
"Nice toss, Seng."

Seng looks curiously over at George. He nods reassuringly back. The overall attitude of the players towards Seng has softened. Carter throws the ball in and the game resumes.

Donavan kneels behind a big brawny BATTER. The pitch races by him. Donavan reaches out for the inside curve, then whips the ball back to Owen on the mound.

The All Stars watch the action, vigilant, ready for anything. Sweat pours out from Seng's hat, but it doesn't distract him from the game.

His eyes shift from the runner on second to the batter at the plate. Owen serves up two more pitches, both of them balls.

Donavan calls a time out, pulls his catcher's mask off and walks out to the mound to confer with Owen. The fans are eager, excited.

Shawn looks on from the announcer's booth. He mops the sweat off his brow with a monogrammed handkerchief.

ANNOUNCER (O.S.)
This heat today seems to have taken its toll on the Maverick's game and the All Stars have taken full advantage of that. Of course the All Stars are used to these conditions. Some of the players spent years working on chain-gangs in sweltering temperatures. The All Stars are in the lead with a score of seven to two.

Donavan returns to his position and the batter steps into the batter's box again.

The runner on second leads off the bag a bit. He seems a little confused. He rubs the perspiration out of his eyes with the back of his hand.

ANNOUNCER (O.S.)

It's no surprise to All Star fans that the star of today's game is Joseph Seng. Seng has been unstoppable. He owns five of the team's seven runs.

The crowd cheers for Seng. His focus stays with the batter. Donovan signals Owen. He winds up and pitches a knuckleball. The batter swings and misses.

Donavan eyes the advancing runner. The man looks faint, pale. Something is definitely not right with him and Seng notices.

Another pitch, another ball. It's a full count. Suddenly the runner on second drops to his knees and falls to the ground, convulsing.

Without hesitating, Seng throws off his glove and rushes over to the man. The runner is shaking violently. He's having a seizure.

Seng grabs the player's shoulders and sits on his chest, pinning his arms to his side. George looks on, stunned. Players from both teams quickly surround the scene.

SENG
(to George)

He's going to bite his tongue off. I need something to put in his mouth.

George frantically looks around on the ground, then over at the Mavericks' third base coach.

GEORGE

We need a pen or a pocket knife over here!!

The coach quickly produces a pencil from his pocket, hurries over to George and hands it to him. George passes the pencil off to Seng and he shoves it into the runner's mouth.

SENG
(stroking man's head)
            Settle down now.

The runner's eyes flutter and roll back in his head. Seng loosens the player's clothing, turns his face sideways and slips his glove underneath his head.

SENG
(shouting)
            Get an ambulance!

The third base coach snaps to and follows Seng's orders.

GEORGE
            Do you know what you're doing?

SENG
(stroking man's head)
            My mother had epilepsy.
(to players around them)
            It's going to be alright.

ANNOUNCER (O.S.)
            The Maverick first baseman Conni Gallup
            is down. Warden Shaw Koslo asks that
            everyone stay seated. Prison guards are
            taking control of the situation.

Several prison GUARDS hurry on to the field and plow through the inmates and players. They corral the prisoners and lead them at gunpoint back to the dugout.

Seng refuses to leave the runner. He wipes the sweat off the man's head with the tail of his uniform. The runner has calmed down some. One of the guards pokes the barrel of a gun into Seng's ribs.

GUARD
            Let's go, Seng.

Just then an ambulance speeds onto the field. MEDICS hop out and race towards the runner. His convulsions have subsided. Seng continues to stroke his head.

SENG

> You're going to be okay.

1ST MEDIC

> Did you put this pencil in his mouth?

SENG

> Yeah.

2ND MEDIC

> Fast thinking.

The medics place the player on a stretcher and load him into the ambulance. Without thinking, Seng starts to follow them inside the vehicle.

Byron steps out from behind the cluster of armed guards and places his hand on Seng's shoulder.

BYRON

> Where do you think you're going?

The guards lead Seng off the field at gunpoint. The Mavericks' COACH walks over to him on his way to the ambulance.

COACH
(sincerely)

> Thank you.

ANNOUNCER (O.S.)

> It's all right, folks. Everything is
> under control.

The nervous crowd settle down a bit. The guards leave Seng to the other teammates, now being shackled. The Mavericks filter off the field. They nod at Seng as the pass and tip their hats to him.

Seng is moved. He swallows a lump in his throat. This is an acceptance he's never known and he's awash in a wave of emotion.

Scene Four

EXT: PRISON YARD—BASEBALL FIELD—DAY

A huge CROWD rings the stands; lines stream from a make-shift ticket window. A crude scoreboard behind left field reads: All Stars 3, Colorado Spyders 3.

It's the bottom of the eighth. The All Stars have two out. The air is thick with excited tension.

The All Stars watch the game from the dugout. They all avoid Seng as he exits the bench. He pretends not to notice or care. He walks to the batter's box picks up a bat and heads for home plate.

ANNOUNCER (O.S.): *The score remains tied at three runs each with the All Stars at bat. With two outs, shortstop Joseph Seng steps up to the plate. Seng is one of the finest all-around players this baseball fan has seen in a long time.*

The crowd cheers for Seng as he squares off against the Spyder's PITCHER. The CATCHER smacks the inside of his glove while casting a menacing glance up at Seng.

CATCHER: (shouting to the pitcher) *Serve 'em up, Zak. This Jailbird ain't going anywhere but back to the cell.* (to Seng) *Ain't that right, jailbird?*

Seng ignores him. The pitcher delivers—Seng strides. Curveball. He swings and misses, off stride. Strike one. The catcher waves the ball in Seng's face.

CATCHER: *This ball scare you, convict?*

SENG: *You want to eat that ball, keep waving it in my face.*

The catcher pulls the mask off his face and stands toe to toe with Seng. Several MEMBERS of the Spyders hustle in from the field to join the disagreement.

CATCHER: *You don't scare me, jailbird.* SENG: *That's too bad. I had hoped you were smarter than you looked.*

The Spyder players surround the pair and the umpire forces himself in between the men, attempting to stop a fistfight before it starts. Seng is in this alone. The All Star players aren't coming to his side.

The catcher looks over at the All Star bench and chuckles. Seng surveys the scene.

CATCHER: *Hope you didn't need any help*

SENG: (coolly) *To handle a piece of s___ like you?*

The umpire nudges the catcher aside and squares off with Seng.

UMPIRE: *You want to play ball or do I have one of the guards shoot you where you stand?*

The Spyders laugh at the situation as they resume their positions on the field. Seng looks over at his teammates; they avert their eyes. They don't give a s___ about Seng at this point.

The catcher gets down in his stance, Seng takes a practice swing, the pitcher throws. The ball carries in a rising line for a good 300 feet, then begins to descend.

The Spyders' LEFT FIELDER pursues the ball, but it's way over his head. The crowd erupts with applause. Seng round the bases.

None of the All Stars say a word when Seng returns to the dugout. George nods to Jack and he hurries out on deck, grabs a bat and heads for home plate.

Seng watches the pitcher toss a fastball Jack's way. The ball is high and way inside. It beans jack on the head hard. He goes down with a thud. The All Stars are on their feet now, yelling obscenities.

The umpire yells for Jack to "take his base." He's dazed, but tried to pull it together. He hustles as best he can to first.

GEORGE: (shouting to Jack) *Shake it off, Jack.*

Laz Korda steps up to bat. Jack looks on, still shaken, but pretending not to be. Laz quickly strikes out. The All Star fans jeer. Jack shuffles off the field. George meets him at the dugout.

GEORGE: (concerned) *You gonna make it?*

Jack nods then heads over to his position at third. Seng watches him bend down to pick up his glove and almost fall. He jogs over to him.

SENG: *Why don't you sit out this inning?*

JACK: *I can't do that. If it looks like they can do without me . . . they will.*

Seng looks up at the guard shack at Shawn. He knows Jack is right.

JACK: *Give me a hand will you?* SENG: *I've got my own position to cover. You can play.*

JACK: *I don't think I can.*

SENG: (hesitating, then) *What do you want me to do?*

JACK: *Any plays come my way . . .*

Seng quickly contemplates the situation, then finally,

SENG: *I got it.*

Jack forces a smile and the inning begins. The crowd cheers enthusiastically. Seng glances over at the scoreboard. It now reads: All Stars 4, Spyders 3.

EXT: PRISON YARD—DAY

The All Stars are marched off the field. Their hands cuffed and feet shackled. George is at the front of the chain-gang and Jack is right behind him. He's feeling off balance.

ANNOUNCER (O.S.): *And so the All Stars keep the Spyders from scoring and win the game by one run.*

George casts a disgusted glance back at Seng, bringing up the rear. Seng keeps his eyes fixed straight ahead. He can feel the stares and does a good job making us believe he doesn't care what anyone thinks.

GEORGE: *Seng ain't gonna be safe tonight. That rat hit a low point . . . pushing a player out of the way to steal a little glory for himself. I don't know what the hell he was doing out there.*

JACK: *What I asked him to. I'm still seeing double. He saved my ass. Tell the boys that.*

Jack looks pale. He's got a big knot on the side of his head. George looks away, perplexed. He stares at Seng and shakes his head. The guards escort the players off the grounds.

Bibliography

Books

Anonymous. *The Sweet Smell of Sagebrush: A Prisoner's Diary*. Wyoming: Friends of the Old Penitentiary, 1990.

Brown, Dee. *The Westerners*. New York: Holt, Rinehart and Winston, 1974.

Brown, Larry. *The Petticoat Prisoners of the Wyoming Frontier. Prison*. Wyoming State Penitentiary: High Plains Press, 1995.

Burns, Ken, and Geoffrey C. Ward. *Baseball An Illustrated History*. New York: Knopf, 2000.

Hanks, Stephen. *The Baseball Chronicle*. Lincolnwood, IL: PIL Publications, 2003.

Stout, Russell E. *100 Years in the Wild West*. Wyoming: Rawlins Newspaper, Inc., 1968.

Ward, Geoffrey C. *The West*. Boston: Little, Brown and Co., 1996.

Newspapers and Periodicals

Brown, Larry. "Batter Up, Body Down." *True West Magazine*. July 2002.

The American Magazine. June 1910.

Woman's Home Companion. May 1911.

The Daily Transcript. Nevada City, California October 20, 1910.

Rawlins Republican. 20 July 1911.

Carbon County Journal. 21 July 1911.

Carbon County Journal. 18 August 1911.

Interviews

Hill, Tina. Site Director, Wyoming Frontier Prison. Rawlins, Wyoming. July 20, 2003.

Evers, Lowell. Wyoming Territory Historian. October 2001.

Correspondence

To Chris Enss From Rans Baker at Carbon County Museum Rawlins, Wyoming. August 29, 2003.

To Chris Enss From Holly Geist at Wyoming State Archives Cheyenne, Wyoming. December 2003.

To Chris Enss From Cindy Brown at Wyoming Department of State Parks and Cultural Resources Cheyenne, Wyoming. July 17, 2002.